DUEL OF ANGELS

by the same author

TIGER AT THE GATES

Jean Giraudoux

DUEL OF ANGELS

(POUR LUCRÈCE)

Translated by

CHRISTOPHER FRY

New York

OXFORD UNIVERSITY PRESS

1959

Printed in the United States of America

DUEL OF ANGELS

NOTE

In performance at the Theatre Royal, Newcastle upon Tyne, the following changes were made in the text:

From page 12, line 9 to page 13, line 10 was omitted, and the following was substituted: ARMAND (*turns to* PAOLA *and turns back in great fury*). But my wife hasn't deceived me.

On page 16, lines 2–10 were omitted.

On page 17, lines 23–30 were omitted, and the following was substituted:

EUGÉNIE. Here he is back again.

ARMAND. Yes. I'm back. When men have been talking to a woman they want to see again, they leave their gloves or their stick behind. I left my life on your table, my dear Eugénie, my entire life.

EUGÉNIE. You left your gloves as well. They would have been quite enough.

On page 42, from line 16, "Poor Paola . . ." to line 24 ". . . light of unhappiness" was omitted.

ACT I

At Aix-en-Provence. About 1868. A summer's day. The terrace of a tea-shop under the lime trees.

(COUNT MARCELLUS. JOSEPH. CUSTOMERS)

JOSEPH. What would you like, sir?

MARCELLUS. What would I like, Joseph? I should like you to tell me what Vice means.

JOSEPH. I left school too young to be able to tell you that, sir.

MARCELLUS. Make a guess. If someone mentions vice to you, what do you imagine?

JOSEPH. We are not here to imagine things, sir; we're here to serve our customers.

MARCELLUS. Then you'd better serve me with whatever goes well with vice. Mr. Justice Blanchard has just proclaimed in open court that I am vice, Joseph.

JOSEPH. I don't really know what to suggest I bring you, sir. Though I always think a mixed ice goes quite well with anything. If you'll excuse me, sir, I'll refer to the manager.

(Exit JOSEPH)

GILLY *(a flower-seller)*. Would you like a flower, sir?

MARCELLUS. No, my dear. You haven't got the flower there which Mr. Justice Blanchard has prescribed for me.

GILLY. I've got some camellias.

MARCELLUS. Mr. Justice Blanchard has insisted that from now on my buttonhole should carry an orchid streaked with blood, stinking of corruption.

GILLY. Antirrhinums, I could manage. That's the nearest we can get to orchids in Aix. It won't take me five minutes to get them for you, sir.

MARCELLUS. Splendid. Bring them to my house.

GILLY. I can't do that, sir. Mr. Justice Blanchard has forbidden any girls under sixteen, especially flower-girls and

1

laundrymaids, to go to the houses of unmarried gentlemen alone, sir.

MARCELLUS. Bring your mother. We can install her in the kitchen.

GILLY. My mother's in prison. Mr. Justice Blanchard sent her there, for taking some letters from the city treasurer to the prefect's wife.

(*Enter* PAOLA *with her husband* ARMAND)

PAOLA. Good afternoon, Vice! Shall we sit next to Vice, Armand?

MARCELLUS. So you've heard about it already.

PAOLA. Beauty is always the first to hear about the sins of the world.

ARMAND. I was in court.

MARCELLUS. I understand he took me to task in no uncertain terms.

ARMAND. Smote you hip and thigh. He was sentencing that girl who used to visit you, who killed her baby.

PAOLA. And he declared our dear city of Aix to be as bad as Sodom or Gomorrah.

MARCELLUS. But what did he say about me? Tell me what he said.

PAOLA. He said they can't imprison you for debt, because you're too rich. They can't run you out of the district for being a nuisance, because you're too wily. No family is going to complain about you, because you would threaten them with blackmail.

ARMAND. But he took it upon himself to execrate your name at the bar of justice, and to point out your face for anyone to spit at who cares to.

MARCELLUS. A very detailed report. To spit at, he said?

ARMAND. That's what he said. He also mentioned debauchery. He also mentioned vice.

MARCELLUS. Precisely in that tone of voice.

ARMAND. I've been an actor in my time. I know how to copy an inflection. He said he had a mission to perform: to see that this town didn't run downhill to perdition, and since you stand for a kind of symbol of the town, he would start his attack with you.

MARCELLUS. I might be listening to the voice of any husband in Aix. I might be listening to you.

ARMAND. I don't mind you thinking so.

PAOLA. Oh, come now, Armand. You don't really side with these hypocrites!

ARMAND. My dear Paola, I'm a husband. You mustn't expect me to congratulate a seducer. You'd better get out of Aix, Marcellus. And I suggest that you hurry.

(JOSEPH *returns*)

JOSEPH. Vice is the natural propensity to evil, sir. We have a dictionary in the office. And the manager advises sherry with a drop of grenadine. That was the strongest thing he remembers them serving at the Café Anglais. But he would like you to be so very good as to choose another table. This one is reserved, sir.

MARCELLUS. For whom, Joseph?

JOSEPH. I don't know, sir.

MARCELLUS. You do know, Joseph. I heard the hesitation. For whom?

JOSEPH. For Madame Lionel Blanchard.

MARCELLUS. For Mr. Justice Blanchard's wife?

PAOLA. Of course, Marcellus. The wife of the man who has given you all this publicity. She comes here every day.

MARCELLUS. The gift of an opportunity; the duel can begin. Have you got a drum, Joseph?

JOSEPH. We have this Egyptian gong, sir.

MARCELLUS. Strike it.

ARMAND. Bad behaviour again, Marcellus!

MARCELLUS. Maybe; but beautifully expressed, as you shall see!

(JOSEPH *beats the gong.* MARCELLUS *rises*)

CUSTOMER. Joseph, we shall all have to leave. That's enough of this racket.

ANOTHER CUSTOMER. If we have to have Vice among us, at least he ought to keep quiet.

MARCELLUS. Forgive me, and stay where you are, honest inhabitants of Aix. Vice has a mission to perform today, and no man alive is going to make him relinquish it. His mission is to introduce Virtue to you; Virtue is on her way. You will see her in the flesh, sitting enthroned in this chair. Give her your careful attention. She can revive your drooping senses far more effectively than Vice can. You will see her, Monsieur Oscar, tasting an ice with a tongue which has never ventured beyond the kiss of a dutiful wife. You will hear her, Monsieur Julius, speaking with a mouth which has never told an untruth. You will watch her picking up a biscuit with fingers which have never strayed away in the dark, my dear Armand.

ARMAND. Kindly leave me out of this.

MARCELLUS. But above all, virtuous wives and excellent husbands of Aix, her coming here will throw light on your own marriages. Wherever this lady goes, life takes on the agreeable charm of the Last Judgement. I don't know how it is, considering she never listens to gossip, but one touch of human frailty and she knows it, and, as far as she's concerned, that's the end of you. Watch her closely. I can tell you, she is absolutely unmerciful. If she refuses to acknowledge an acquaintance, you can be quite sure that acquaintance has found a lover . . .

ARMAND. Here she is, I think, Marcellus. You'd better shut up.

MARCELLUS. If she suddenly refuses to speak to some poor husband, his wife has betrayed him; and any husband so betrayed she holds personally responsible.

PAOLA. That's enough, Marcellus. You're being tiresome.

MARCELLUS. Don't hesitate. Use this touchstone to show you what you are yourselves. Try asking her for the sugar; if you've just been reading the *Decameron* she won't pass it. Pick up her scarf; she won't accept it from you if she knows you've got a collection of rather light-hearted engravings. Here she is. Go and meet her, Joseph. You'll be able to tell from the way she greets you whether you're deceived or deceiving.

PAOLA. Let's change our table. Let's go over there.

ARMAND. Why?

MARCELLUS. Here she comes, to take over from me. Vice and Virtue are meeting face to face for the first time. Her expression will tell you, fellow inhabitants of Aix, what part I'm expected to play for the rest of the afternoon.

(LUCILE *enters with* EUGÉNIE)

MARCELLUS. This is your table, madam. I have been keeping it for you.

LUCILE (*smiling at him*). Thank you.

(MARCELLUS *goes to a distant table*)

LUCILE. Good afternoon, Joseph. You're bowing very low today.

JOSEPH. Slightly lower than yesterday, madam. I have good reason to.

LUCILE. But you'll bring us our ices, won't you, Joseph?

JOSEPH. I shall see they're even colder than yesterday, madam.

LUCILE. And the chocolate a little hotter, I hope.

JOSEPH. The ice freezing, madam. The chocolate boiling.

LUCILE. Perfect.

JOSEPH (*coming back to her*). My wife makes the wafers.

LUCILE. Thank her very much. Remember me to her, Joseph.

JOSEPH. Thank you, madam, I will! I shall kiss her, madam. My goodness, I'm delighted.

(*Exit* JOSEPH)

LUCILE. Are you sulking, Eugénie?

EUGÉNIE. Yes, I am. I'm vexed that you didn't let Guy come with us.

LUCILE. I never feel quite at ease with him. I'm afraid I can't help it.

EUGÉNIE. There's beginning to be a lot of talk in the town about your likes and dislikes. They're so extraordinary.

LUCILE. What do you mean?

EUGÉNIE. Well, you don't seem to have any particular aversion to thieves. Or drunkards; I've seen you being most pleasant to them. Even that murderer we saw being arrested; you looked as though you pitied him.

LUCILE. He was much to be pitied. And my husband is the judge. One judge in the family is enough.

EUGÉNIE. You can face any of these faults and crimes quite cheerfully, be talkative, and gracious, and in the best of spirits. Then you suddenly freeze and clench your teeth and refuse to speak, as though your flesh had been turned to stone.

LUCILE. But you know why.

EUGÉNIE. Yes, I do. Someone in love had just happened to go past.

LUCILE. That's far from the truth.

EUGÉNIE. Some enchanting woman was going by on her way to see her lover. Or a young man waved to us when he was running to fetch a letter from the poste restante.

LUCILE. Are you lying to hurt me, or just for the sake of lying?

EUGÉNIE. A woman can be swathed up to the neck, as modestly as possible. You still manage to discover the marks of unlawful kissing hidden away on her body. It's as though when you looked at a wealth of family jewellery your eyes saw nothing except the fake. You're making this town impossible to live in.

LUCILE. What does it have to do with the town?

EUGÉNIE. Aix was like a town of love before you came here. At least half the road these people took through life was dedicated to love. And what a beautiful pattern their footsteps made, lacing and interlacing! If you followed any man or woman in Aix at any time of the day or night they would bring you to where love was.

LUCILE. That's a strange name to give it.

EUGÉNIE. The right one. Desire, pursuit, jealousy, blessing, despair—love can be called by any of them.

LUCILE. Not by me. Love is called love, and no other name will do.

EUGÉNIE. It gave a great many privileges to this town: husbands were trusting, mothers were careful to shut their eyes. Even the smallest, ordinary pleasures came brilliantly to life because they happened in a world of love. As though the climate of Aix bred love like a fever, and nobody minded. We left typhoid and cholera to Marseilles; here we had love. And then you came along, you and your judge of a husband, Lucile and Lionel.

LUCILE. Lucile and Lionel, who simply love each other, without complication.

EUGÉNIE. They arrived from Limousin, the country which has bred more Popes and fewer lovers than any other in the world. And Lionel has been a success, both as a jealous husband and an upright judge. From the first month he was here he picked up the threads of every affair in the town. And his homilies rang out, his sermons against public licence, and off to the pillory went all the happy people who were guilty. People laugh at him, because they understand what he doesn't understand. But you, Lucile, really did bring calamity with you.

LUCILE. I brought calamity?

(JOSEPH *returns*)

JOSEPH. Your ices, madam.

LUCILE. Thanks.

JOSEPH. My wife sends you these wafers with her compliments.

LUCILE. Thanks.

JOSEPH. My wife –

EUGÉNIE. Stop worrying us about your wife, Joseph.

JOSEPH. Oh, dear! It's what I was afraid of!

(*Exit* JOSEPH)

EUGÉNIE. You've given the taste of hell to innocent, carefree pleasure. They believe you're guilty of reintroducing original sin: you needn't suppose you're another Lucrece. You're the angel of evil.

LUCILE. And yet it's all so simple.

EUGÉNIE. What is it you see about these people which suddenly turns you to stone?

LUCILE. I see insects and reptiles on them.

EUGÉNIE. A peculiar gift.

LUCILE. I realize perfectly well that if I were a saint I shouldn't despise them for it. But I can't help it. On every incontinent person I see a creature.

EUGÉNIE. Always the same creature?

LUCILE. No. It may be slimy, or it may be crawling. It comes out of their mouths, and runs over their bodies.

EUGÉNIE. And all this time you have been seeing one on my friend Guy?

LUCILE. A little one. A very little toad. Hardly more than a tadpole.

EUGÉNIE. In his hand, when you refused to shake hands with him?

LUCILE. No; on his mouth.

EUGÉNIE. You haven't come from Limousin; you've come out of the Middle Ages. And did you see one on Clotilda when you hurried past without speaking to her?

LUCILE. There was a maggot in the corner of her eye.

EUGÉNIE. Can you say this without laughing? And if there should happen to be someone you think well of, what do you see on them?

LUCILE. I see their senses lying transparent under their skin. Their eyes are like clear water. Their bones like ivory.

EUGÉNIE. Your morality is uncommonly physical, it seems to me.

LUCILE. Our bodies are what God has given into our keeping, Eugénie. He takes care of our souls himself.

EUGÉNIE. I'm surprised that you've noticed your body. Have you really been daring enough to look at it in the mirror? Don't you tie yourself up in a sack when you sleep with the judge?

LUCILE. I have a great respect for my body. It is healthy, loyal, and sensible. I keep well away from that common burial ground which promiscuity leads to. Who are you smiling at?

EUGÉNIE. At Paola. Acknowledge her. She's waving to you.

LUCILE. Never.

EUGÉNIE. Don't be difficult; please, Lucile. Paola is great fun, and very beautiful. You needn't wave, but incline your head to her beauty.

LUCILE. Beauty which takes a lover isn't there for me to see.

EUGÉNIE. A slug is crawling out of her ear, I suppose?

LUCILE. Praying mantises; thousands of them.

EUGÉNIE. Her husband is smiling at you, very insistently.

LUCILE. A man whose wife takes a lover doesn't smile; he makes an insulting grimace.

EUGÉNIE. But he doesn't know anything about it. You know Armand. Only this morning you were speaking very well of him. If he guessed he would kill himself, or kill somebody.

LUCILE. Why, everything must surely shout it at him. If he can't detect it in the whole atmosphere of his house, then he's as guilty and contemptible as all the rest are.

EUGÉNIE. Be careful. He'll see it in your face.

LUCILE. My face makes it useless to try to lie. That's why sometimes I can look at it in the mirror.

EUGÉNIE. Please, Lucile; do acknowledge them. He has gone quite pale, and Paola is furious. Armand knows perfectly well what makes you refuse to recognize a friend, what it is that strikes you dumb in front of a husband.

LUCILE. Dumb, deaf, and blind.

EUGÉNIE. He is coming over to us. Say something to him, just a word or two. I'm not asking you to touch him.

LUCILE. There isn't any difference; if I speak it's as if I touched him. And anyway, after this conversation love is the only word on my tongue at the moment. Don't ask me to speak to him.

EUGÉNIE. Poor Armand! He always talks like a lyric poet, and now here he comes, searching for his death.

(ARMAND *reaches the table*)

ARMAND. My respects to you, dear madam.

EUGÉNIE. Thank you, dear Armand. We accept them.

ARMAND. My respects, Eugénie . . . You also accept them, I hope, Madame Blanchard? It is wonderful to see you together, two women endued with the same grace.

EUGÉNIE. We go to the same dressmaker, my dear friend.

ARMAND. Really wonderful: as though grace couldn't completely express itself without the help of two such different souls and bodies.

EUGÉNIE. You could hardly say more if you wrote a sonnet to us, Armand.

ARMAND. But it's not so satisfactory to think it should have provided only one voice between you. Two mouths, but one voice.

EUGÉNIE. Some men would think that was a very reasonable arrangement for women.

ARMAND. And yet I wish that your friend could have told me why she doesn't make any acknowledgement when Paola waves to her.

EUGÉNIE. I don't think she saw her.

ARMAND. Then I wish she could tell me why Paola has become invisible to her, twenty feet away, in a red dress, and smiling all over her face in this direction. Paola has just given the biggest smile of her life.

EUGÉNIE. You should be very thankful that my friend is so lost in abstraction. Otherwise she would see the most charming man in Aix becoming importunate.

ARMAND. I'm only saying what all Aix is feeling. The town is deeply disturbed by Madame Blanchard's attacks of blindness and deafness.

EUGÉNIE. We're very sorry; there's no cure, I'm afraid.

ARMAND. I think there is. They say that Madame Blanchard would talk from dawn to dusk without a pause, and even chatter on into her dreams, if every couple in the town were perfect.

EUGÉNIE. I don't understand what you mean.

ARMAND. Yes, you do; but you're the one entrusted to speak, so you're also the one entrusted to lie. And as I have to use you as an interpreter, tell your friend that I'm begging her to break the silence. If she doesn't speak to me, she's forcing me to believe that either I'm an unfaithful husband or a deceived one. But I know I'm a faithful husband . . .

EUGÉNIE. Are you sure of that?

ARMAND. You can't wave the charges away. I've been meaning for a long time to shout from the rooftops that I love my wife. It isn't often done, to trumpet abroad a husband's love for his wife, particularly in Aix. I'm grateful to your friend for giving me the chance.

EUGÉNIE. Don't shout so loud. Your wife is looking.

ARMAND. I hope she can hear me. I love my wife in and above everything. Don't smile. You don't have to speak simply when you make a public confession; you want words that resound. Thanks to her, I love everything. Thanks to her, I have everything. The world, and time, and space, have surrendered to me by way of her. In her I move, in her I breathe. For me she is every minute on the clock. She's the sun in the sky; the whole solar system. My wife is the only reason I love at all. And now perhaps you can see why I should like Madame Blanchard to speak to me . . .

EUGÉNIE. You're insisting so much. It discourages conversation.

ARMAND.   . . . to say any word she likes. Let Madame Blanchard mention the weather to me. Let her ask me if it's going to be fine. She will see then. Eugénie, the sky will never have looked so wonderfully promising.

EUGÉNIE. We were talking about the weather when you came over to us. There's nothing more to say about it.

ARMAND. I'm not asking for charity, I don't want her to lie.

EUGÉNIE. Now listen, Armand! At last a woman has come into this distracted world who refuses to speak when she has nothing to say, who likes to be allowed to become a statue if she wants to, and you pester her with idiotic questions!

ARMAND. Even a statue would answer me, at the moment.

EUGÉNIE. If Lucile gave in to you, it would be because she thought you were stupid. All she could say to you would be that you're like everybody else, pigheaded and egotistical, incapable of understanding the heart and the silence it longs to have.

ARMAND. Very well: I withdraw. Madame Blanchard needn't be silent any longer . . . Thank you, madam.

(*He goes back to his wife*)

EUGÉNIE. You can now congratulate yourself that you kept the word love safe in your mouth like an acid drop.

LUCILE. It hasn't melted.

EUGÉNIE. And suppose now he should slap Paola's face in public, would you condescend to tell him he had done well? Or suppose he should kill her?

LUCILE. There's no fear of that. He was acting a part.

EUGÉNIE. But she certainly isn't. And she's going to make sure that you know that. Poor Armand! What have you been doing this morning to make you so cruel to husbands?

LUCILE. Nothing much. I kissed my husband, and held him in my arms when he set off on circuit to Draguignan. I washed a dinner service of old Marseilles china. I read two metaphysical poems. Then I sat down and wrote a letter to my husband, telling him that I had washed the dinner service and read the poems.

EUGÉNIE. Here he is back again.

ARMAND. Yes. I'm back. When men have been talking to a woman they want to see again, they leave their gloves or their stick behind. I left my life on your table, my dear Eugénie, my entire life.

EUGÉNIE. You left your gloves as well. They would have been quite enough.

ARMAND (*taking the gloves*). Thank you.

EUGÉNIE. And now I suppose you want to look for your life?

ARMAND. I've already seen it. My wife hasn't deceived me.

EUGÉNIE. Dear heaven, what are we talking about?

ARMAND. About my wife. She hasn't deceived me. I've come back to ask Madame Blanchard why she won't speak.

EUGÉNIE. Madame Blanchard has to recite two metaphysical poems at the Archbishop's reception tomorrow afternoon. This is the only time she has to go over them in her mind. Don't worry her.

ARMAND. I see. And I'm sure Madame Blanchard has also sworn to count up to a million, and she would have to start all over again if she interrupted herself. But my wife hasn't deceived me.

EUGÉNIE. Then she should have done. You're impossible.

ARMAND. I'm a visionary, in a way. I've often foreseen death, and accidents, and people's good fortune. But I've never felt any apprehensiveness when I thought of Paola. Very often I hear myself talking out loud to myself in the street, and I tell myself hard truths which had never occurred to me before. But I've never heard myself say: 'Your wife has a lover, Armand. You have a wife who has a lover.' And that's because she hasn't.

EUGÉNIE. If you don't stop, Armand, we shall have to leave.

ARMAND. No, you won't. Madame Blanchard has no intention of leaving. She's not the sort of person to beat a retreat, or compromise. She keeps her opinions to herself, even if it kills her. But there's no reason why she should; and I'll tell her why. I am very like her. I shrink away from unpleasantness and uncertainty, and, like her, I'm speechless when I come across deception and the sins of the flesh. I know I might very well overlook an excess of sentiment or imagination in my wife, but never a fault of her body. I've just been testing this now, sitting beside her. She drank her coffee like an innocent woman; she broke her biscuit like a faithful wife. She took a sip of water like a woman who had never known, or seen, or touched any man except her husband.

EUGÉNIE. Who doubts it? No one ever questioned it!

ARMAND. I certainly don't. Besides, if my wife wasn't faithful, I should have known it an hour ago. I go back to my house once a day unexpectedly and I quietly open the door, not to take Paola by surprise, of course, God forbid, but to surprise the house itself. And that's what I did just now. My proof is less than an hour old. All I surprised was a complete innocence. You know I collect furniture; and I know if anything were ever wrong, those beautiful, various pieces, the rosewood and acacia-wood, and so on, would seem to me to be all made of the same dreary material, common wood, like the common flesh of mankind. But just now the walnut still came from the walnut tree, the rosewood from the rose. And in my collection of Turkish bric-a-brac the coiling and glittering snakes of pure silver were pure silver still, and still delighted my heart. The tranquil waters of Europe still flowed for me, the peaceful waters of Asia still sang in my ear. So you see, Eugénie . . .

EUGÉNIE. So don't insist, Armand.

ARMAND. I'm not insisting. I've always taken care not to insist. But there's one other thing I want to tell Madame Blanchard, which she doesn't know. I created Paola. I created her temperament, her wit, and all her ways of living. She has read nothing but what I have read, and seen only the pictures and the landscapes which I showed her. Not because she wasn't capable of doing these things for herself; in every way she's both gifted and original. But she chose to let herself be created by me. She eats and drinks according to my taste, dresses and undresses according to my taste. I made her days, her nights, even her flesh. It would be wise of Madame Blanchard to believe that I don't create a woman just to be betrayed by her.

EUGÉNIE. My dear Armand, do be serious. Sit down here, next to us. Let me offer you an ice.

ARMAND. There; that's all. I won't ask Madame Blanchard to say a word. You were quite right just now, Eugénie. It's quite natural that a woman should suddenly find it tiresome to speak; tiresome and complicated.

EUGÉNIE. You're becoming quite sensible.

ARMAND. Good-bye, madam. I am going back to fidelity, love, and happiness. I shall never leave them again.

EUGÉNIE. Till tomorrow, Armand.

ARMAND (*turning back*). However, there's one favour I should like to ask of Madame Blanchard. It may be impossibly difficult for her to speak, but it's easy enough to drink. Perfectly pleasant to raise a glass of water to the mouth. If Madame Blanchard agrees to tell me, without words, that I'm right, let her simply raise her glass to her lips. May I tell her that it's a very hot day, and she may enjoy it.

EUGÉNIE. Till tomorrow, Armand.

> (ARMAND *looks at* LUCILE, *who does not drink. He goes away. As soon as he has gone,* LUCILE *unconsciously raises her glass to her lips.* ARMAND, *who is still looking at her, sees this, and his face lights up.*
>
> *She breaks the glass.* ARMAND *closes his eyes – confounded*)

EUGÉNIE. You know what you're doing, don't you? You're stirring up scandal, and a tragic drama. Armand was a magnificent peacock with a hundred blind eyes in his tail. Now you're making those eyes able to see.

LUCILE. Good. I hope they see everything.

EUGÉNIE. Putting a husband on his guard is like letting loose the sorcerer's apprentice. In a flash Armand is going to see every one of Paola's lovers, one for each eye. He will ruin her, destroy her completely.

LUCILE. If she deserves it, where's the harm?

EUGÉNIE. Life is very hard for women like Paola. What they would really like is to be virgin for each new lover. But they have twenty loves, and only one body.

LUCILE. They have twenty bodies, and no love whatsoever.

EUGÉNIE. It maddens me to listen to you professing virtue in a tea-shop, like a martyr professing his faith in the arena. It's in bad taste, and with a tigress like Paola, it's dangerous.

LUCILE. You make me sound ridiculous when you say 'virtue'. What have I said that has anything to do with being virtuous?

EUGÉNIE. Well, purity, if you like.

LUCILE. A beautiful word.

EUGÉNIE. Words have no connexion with all this.

LUCILE. For me they have. And I will tell you which words; words like fountain, spring-water, crystal, and clarity. Don't try and make me pity a disloyal wife and an unperceiving husband, when there are words like truth and innocence. You should imitate me a little, trust less to your thoughts and more to language. That's why I can be glad to open my eyes every morning. A flight of pure words lifts me into the sunshine.

EUGÉNIE. The word love isn't so ugly.

LUCILE. I'm very sure it isn't. Tell Armand so. I have cleansed it for him; you will see the strength it has now.

(*A* STOUT MAN *has got up from his table, and crosses to the two women. He drops on one knee beside them, and pretends to fasten his shoe-lace*)

MAN. Help me to speak to you without being noticed, ladies. I'm the mace-bearer at the commercial court. This is very serious.

EUGÉNIE. Pretend to be searching for a gold piece.

MAN. I'd better look for a franc. It would seem more natural.

EUGÉNIE. Well? What is it?

MAN. Madame Blanchard, do speak to M. Armand. He's a very admirable man. You're killing him.

EUGÉNIE. It may be here, under the table.

MAN. What may, Madame Eugénie?

EUGÉNIE. Not my nose, your franc . . . Go on.

MAN. Madame Paola had an enemy once before, someone as beautiful as you are, who tried to take away her husband.

EUGÉNIE. But that isn't what we are doing.

MAN. You are. You're not taking him away for yourself, but you're taking him away from her. The person I'm referring to had to suffer for it. Someone unknown saw that she was well punished. It wouldn't have been surprising if her body had been scarred for life, if only one cheek and one eye had been left for her to look at in the mirror.

EUGÉNIE. Is this all you have to say?

MAN. By no means. I could tell you three other similar stories. But my back is breaking. It's most difficult, finding a franc you haven't lost. Ah, here it is. Many thanks, ladies. (*He goes*)

EUGÉNIE. You heard that. Now, please. Armand will come back again. Everything that man said about Paola is true. She's inexorable. Speak to her husband. Or else let us leave here.

LUCILE. That man came just at the right moment. Otherwise I might have left.

EUGÉNIE. You mean you insist on staying.

LUCILE. Don't you ever feel that you've been given sometimes a direct order, something wills you to go to the house-keeper's room when you were really going to the drawing-room or up to the attic? My natural instinct now is to go home; there's some jam to be made and the laundry to see to. But my secret orders tell me to stay where I am.

EUGÉNIE. All right, let's stay, then. We shall discover what part obstinacy plays in this sad world.

LUCILE. We shall discover what part dignity plays in the human scheme.

(ARMAND *re-enters*)

ARMAND. Madame Blanchard has found her voice again, I notice. The metaphysical poems have been rehearsed. She has counted up to a million. So I've come back.

EUGÉNIE. As we see. For the third time.

ARMAND. That's not many. I've seen a cat that was being drowned come back to shore twelve times, in spite of the sticks. Men haven't got the same tenacity. There will be no fourth time.

EUGÉNIE. My friend was showing you that a woman can be just as obstinate as a man, and more. You have lost. Let's call the game finished.

ARMAND. Well, Madame Blanchard spoke. And her voice was charming. But I'm sorry she did. When I sat over there listening to her, I noticed an imperfection in my wife which I had

never noticed before. I always thought Paola had a gentle
voice; low and gentle. But Paola's voice is hard, rasping. I
used to think how firm and beautiful her lips were when she
spoke, a heavenly horizontal. But they're not. They twist,
and snap. Until today she sang like a lark; but what sort of
croaking raven will she be tonight, I wonder.

EUGÉNIE. This was what my friend was trying to spare you
when she wouldn't speak. So much the worse for you.

ARMAND. Then it was just as wrong for your friend to look
at me. Madame Blanchard has eyes which have shown me
that Paola's eyes aren't velvet, as I thought they were, but
more like steel. I'm thankful I haven't felt Madame Blanchard's hand, or what would become of Paola's skin, which
has always seemed to make the days and nights pass over me
smooth as silk. A few minutes ago I touched it. It was still
smooth, but it sweated a little – from fear, I think.

EUGÉNIE. If you won't leave now, Lucile, I shall go alone.
This is sheer cruelty.

ARMAND. And yet Paola was so very dear to me until this
morning. Madame Blanchard can have no idea what her
tenderness used to be. I can remember so many things, which
are very revealing. The care she took not to wake me; how
she would slip into my arms without disturbing me when she
came back from those solitary midnight visits she so loved
making, to a church where the incense had the smell of
tobacco; I noticed how the smell of it clung to her. And how,
when it rained, her shoes would still be miraculously dry,
because one of the saints had carried her home. It was a
church where they gave red roses to the faithful, and she
always chose the two most perfect roses to put in a vase by
my side. I could smell the scent of them all through the
night. And how brave she was, how she would hide from me
the scratches and bruises she was so often giving herself. She
would bruise her shoulders, and her breasts . . . just like a
child . . . Sometimes even her belly. Oh God, I don't
know!

EUGÉNIE (*getting up*). You're both going mad, both of you,

you who can't stop talking, and my friend who refuses to speak at all; you're both losing your senses.

ARMAND. Not at all. On the contrary. It seems to me I'm finding them again. Give the devil his due. A clear vision; a twofold vision. Behind Madame Blanchard I can see an angel, her exact counterpart, suffering herself to be silent, forming a word with her lips, the unexpected word of friendship. And behind my wife a kind of monster, with drooping eyelids, yet looking so like her, and speaking the strange word 'hatred'.

EUGÉNIE. Are you contented now, Lucile? This is your doing.

ARMAND. Yes, her doing. Or rather, not her doing. Because I've been watching my wife and I know she has lied to me.

EUGÉNIE. Do you see a crawling creature on me, Lucile? You don't, I think. And that's because your peculiar gift is absolutely false. I have a lover. Good-bye.

(*Exit* EUGÉNIE)

ARMAND. I'm glad she has gone. You didn't speak because she was here, isn't that so? And, because she was here, I talked too much, isn't that it? She has a lover. What can we do? Human beings are human beings. Whether it's a great herd of stags coming away from their offices at six, or out of their clubs and cafés at eight; or a great herd of females collected together in the wash-house or the tea-shop, what can we do? The human animal is promiscuous. What I find so unjust is that I should have the feeling of having failed, or of having killed something. If the innocent are to suffer remorse, the guilty, presumably, should feel aggrieved. It's the worst possible solution.

PAOLA (*from her table*). Armand!

ARMAND. I came into this place with a young, faithful, beautiful wife; with memories of days which were happy, without spot or blemish; I leave with a graceless wife, whose looks have already gone; with years behind me of being fooled and humiliated. A splendid afternoon's work. I congratulate you. An anonymous silence is worth more than all the anonymous letters that were ever written.

PAOLA (*still from her table*). Armand!

ARMAND. She's calling me. She doesn't hear how harsh her voice is.

LUCILE (*turning to him with tears in her eyes*). Now you must listen to me – I do beg of you to listen!

ARMAND. Well? I'm listening.

LUCILE. You haven't understood what my silence meant.

ARMAND. Have you been silent? It seems to me that we've told each other everything. It's the one profitable thing to have come out of the day. Happiness, misery, men, women: you've told me everything.

LUCILE. Someone told me you had spoken ill of my husband. That is why I've been reserved with you. I wasn't for a moment thinking of Paola.

ARMAND. A lie can be a very lovely thing, when a truthful woman tells it. I should like to see how far you can take it. To ask you to swear that Paola is faithful to me.

LUCILE. I'm quite ready to. What did you say about my husband at the club the day before yesterday?

ARMAND. I said that virtue was the weakness of strong generals, and the strength of weak magistrates.

LUCILE. Don't you think that was infamous? Now leave me. I won't say another word. Go away. Will you please go?

ARMAND. I'm not going back to the house today. I'm afraid of it.

(PAOLA *has got up, and is coming towards them*)

PAOLA. Armand, angel?

ARMAND. Yes?

PAOLA. Angel, go and fetch me my wrap; I'm cold. You wouldn't mind slipping back to the house for it?

ARMAND. All right.

(*Exit* ARMAND)

PAOLA (*to* LUCILE). Will you condescend to speak to me?

LUCILE. That depends on the question.

PAOLA. No question; some information. I've come to tell you what you are.

LUCILE. I already know. I'm someone who can't bear women like you.

PAOLA. Even simpler than that. You're a woman who loves men.

LUCILE. That may be, when they've earned the right to be called men.

PAOLA. Like Charlemagne, for instance? Or Alexander? Or that saint who took such care of the children? I've forgotten his name.

LUCILE. You haven't forgotten it. It's avoiding you.

PAOLA. Much good may it do it. But I'm more honest with myself; I can see them and judge them, without having to make great men out of them first.

LUCILE. One visits where one is received.

PAOLA. Be frank with me. What about other men, such as that swimmer you saw dive naked into the sea the other day: or the tenor we heard singing in *Aïda* last Thurdsay, who seemed to be moulded to his tights? Are they men to you, or not? What place do shoulders, and biceps, and thighs take in your vocabulary?

LUCILE. I've no idea.

PAOLA. You're thirty years old. You will soon find out. When men give themselves away to us: their footsteps on the pavement at night, letting us guess their weight; or their shadows in the moonlight showing us how insubstantial they are; or their voices coming up from the street, loud or gentle; what does all this mean to you? What do you make of it?

LUCILE. Shadows, footsteps, voices. Nothing more than that.

PAOLA. You're lying. They make your life. They're what you love.

LUCILE. Thank you for letting me know.

PAOLA. No thanks to me. You're a fairly rare type, but not unheard of. You're one of the women who never get used to

living among millions of male bodies and souls. Day and
night you're astonished at being a woman. Your reserve, and
apparent modesty, come from this inability to take your sex
for granted. You're curious about the woman you are, and
at the same time rather frightened. You look at her in the
mirror without ever getting to know her. When you're alone
it's as though you'd made a shy arrangement to meet her;
you move anxiously towards her when you're in bed . . .
But that's not how you feel about men; men to you are clear,
complete, and male, in body and spirit; and this game of
virtue you play is nothing but affectation.

LUCILE. You describe yourself very well.

PAOLA. It's no description of me. I'm the complete opposite.
I can never see or love more than one man. Not always the
same one, I admit; I change him, but I love no one else. Not
another man exists in the world. When he is with me, the rest
are invisible, gone clean out of existence. When I love, every
ship sails the sea without sailors, carriages travel without
coachmen, the cakes in this shop make their own way up
from the kitchen. In the confessional I'm given absolution
by an echo. I watch other women dancing in a void, taking
emptiness by the hand, laughing and chattering with what
has no existence; because the only man who has any sub-
stance, flesh, or blood, is in my arms.

LUCILE. Does your husband also go clean out of existence?

PAOLA. My husband? No. He is still there, an obsession, a
vague centre of my consciousness, the agreeable obsession
who is my husband, like a memory which we don't turn to
because we're so occupied with the present time. A com-
panion, more shadow than flesh, who has my everyday life
in his keeping. My interests, and habits, and likes, and dislikes are all safely in his care; my conversation on his lips,
with everything I shall urgently need on the day I give up my
latest lover; so when that awful day comes, the first man to
emerge will be my husband. He will immediately become
substantial, and encourage all the other men to come gradu-
ally out of the void where I had banished them. That's why

I hold on to my husband. And now you know why I don't intend to let you separate us. Where should we find our next lover, without a husband to put men back into the world again?

LUCILE. This is absolutely horrifying!

PAOLA. A respectable remark, but humbug, if I may say so. Your own husband means even less to you than that.

LUCILE. We won't bring my husband into this.

PAOLA. However hard you may try to put the head of Solomon on to the judge, you don't change his body, which means nothing to you at all.

LUCILE. Wicked woman!

PAOLA. Well done. You spit with great charm, like a shocked schoolgirl. Your husband: it makes me laugh to think of him stirring up the woman in you for some other man's benefit. Lionel presenting you to Bertrand, or Jean-Paul, or Guy.

LUCILE. You know a number of Christian names.

PAOLA. Why, you let him go away; of course you don't love your husband. Every week, four times in a month, you're willing to let him go on circuit while you lie in an empty bed, perfectly contented and comfortable, suffering the worst evil that can happen to any woman in love: the absence of the lover. If you could have seen your look of calm well-being when you came in just now, you would have known that your husband meant nothing at all to you.

LUCILE. Oh, Lionel, my dear, forgive me for talking to this woman.

PAOLA. . . . who is teaching you the truth about a woman. Oh, Lionel, my dear, take as much time as you like on your journey! When you're away you're still close to me! . . . Completely untrue! Absence is absence; death, in fact. If someone I love is going away, if only for a day or an hour, I hold him to me, and cry out as though breath was leaving me; I hide his shoes. I make furious faces out of the window at him as he goes away, and insult him. You stand at the window and smile. When his weight is lifted off me, the weight of the world descends. But you breathe freely at last.

LUCILE. I hate you.

PAOLA. Hating another woman doesn't make you love your husband. And now listen to me. There's one thing that we won't leave undecided, and I've come to warn you of it.

LUCILE. Who is 'we'? Are you speaking for some society?

PAOLA. Yes, I am. For all women. We believe that the worst crime any woman can commit is to go over to the side of the men. The one inviolable pact since the creation of the world, has been this agreement between women. And the woman who breaks it is bound for disaster. Man is simple. The only thing he demands from us is peace and quiet, to be left to play with his horses, and his work, and his money, and his own self-importance. He doesn't ask to live a real life, or to nurse his real passions, or to be a reality, in the sense a woman is. He wants to go on with his game of make-believe. Your husband, for instance, is ambitious and hard, but his make-believe is virtue. My husband's as jealous as a tiger; his make-believe is to be completely trusting. So, thanks to their short-sightedness, we run naked through the world, with our senses, and freedom of movement, and pleasures of the body. But if one woman betrays us, and for five minutes gives a man clear sight, they all start being, not *really* indignant and revengeful, but *playing* at indignation and revenge. And they get too carried away by their game to stop short of a scandal.

LUCILE. And so?

PAOLA. So I speak to you without any apology, because I'm speaking for every woman. I have to tell you that we've been watching you very closely for some time. And there are some of us who are not going to tolerate the way you're behaving.

LUCILE. Explain yourself.

PAOLA. The explanations are over. Now I'll prescribe for you. When you see a friend going off to visit her lover, you will give her your hand, and when she's returning, you'll smile at her; you'll talk and laugh with the deceived, indulgent husband. You will make quite sure that what you do won't lead a man into making believe he sees things as they are, and perhaps committing a crime.

LUCILE. Or else?

PAOLA. Or else, nothing. Or else an illustration of the divine law: scandal rebounds on to whoever provokes it. Who draws the sword shall perish by the sword. Who lifts the veil must draw aside the shroud. You can choose your own text. And now, my dear, I can smile at you. It's a long-term smile, you don't have to return it before tomorrow. But you will speak to my husband today, indeed now, because here he is.

LUCILE. I'm quite ready to.

(ARMAND *has come back with a wrap over his arm*)

PAOLA. Armand, Madame Blanchard would like to speak to you.

ARMAND. Unnecessary. I know what Madame Blanchard has to say.

PAOLA. Surely not, darling: surely not.

ARMAND. I'm listening.

LUCILE. You must forgive me for not answering you. It was wrong of me. Silence isn't the way to speak to a man like yourself. Though it may have helped you. Up to now I have given you the silence of a child; now you shall have the words of a woman. I owe this change to your wife. Thank her, as I do. She has made me see that you're not the conceited, hypocritical husband I thought you, but a good and suffering man. If I'm to believe her, a woman is going to speak the truth to a man for the first time. Apparently this means, I am going to betray every woman in the world, but this I don't believe, because it's the only way I can keep faith with myself. I mean by repeating to you, like a traitor, what she has been confiding to me; by telling you, like a spy, her naked secrets. Your wife is a monster. She has been unfaithful to you twenty times over, a hundred times. I'm not talking about the men she calls her lovers, Bertrand or Jean-Paul or Guy. She continually deceives you with every living human being. You're not a man at all to her: you're simply the lay-figure of a man who is there to keep her secure in the love of men when the man she loves is tired of her. Leave her. It's better to have twenty-four hours of truth a day than twenty-four hours of lies. Twenty-four hours of honour instead of twenty-four hours of shame. Leave her; it will give you the chance to re-discover all the things you've been missing for some time, the good opinion of the world, of the natural world, of animals and trees; and, more important still, you will have your own good opinion, and you will have mine.

ARMAND. Very well. It shall be done . . . Good-bye, Paola.

PAOLA. Where are you going?

ARMAND. It's done. It's the easiest thing in the world to change one's life. Thank you, madam.

PAOLA. Armand!

ARMAND. How easy it is! Why, everything that belongs to a married couple knows, of its own accord, how it ought to be divided when the couple separate. I can see just how the household is arranging itself: what things go to you, what animals and which of the servants will want to come with me. How unnecessary lawyers really are.

PAOLA. My dearest, what are you doing?

ARMAND. Oh, all you who are tortured by the knowledge that your wife has a lover, imagine she's not your wife any longer, nor will be your wife any longer, and happiness will come back to you.

PAOLA. Armand!

ARMAND. Here's your wrap, Paola. Put it on. You're stark naked.

(*He goes*)

LUCILE. I'm thirsty!

PAOLA. Your thirst can be quenched with water. You're very lucky.

LUCILE. You should be satisfied now; I've spoken to him.

(*She drinks from a glass into which* PAOLA *has dropped a powder, and makes to go*)

PAOLA. Are you going? Just one moment.

LUCILE. Don't touch me.

PAOLA. Oh yes, I will. When I was a little girl, instead of collecting stamps I had a trick of touching the lips of people I admired or despised. Now I shall add to my collection and touch yours. Why, what's the matter? They're cold.

LUCILE. Let me go.

PAOLA. No. A peculiarity of mine is to measure both the people I love and the people I hate by the same yardstick. They all rouse the same desire in me, to touch them, or better still to hold them. So I hold you. I will let you go when I think fit. A woman with something in her grasp has fingers more tenacious than the jaws of a bulldog.

LUCILE. Whether you let me go or not, I don't belong to your regiment of women.

PAOLA. You don't belong! You will see what happens to a woman who leaves it.

     (LUCILE *faints.* JOSEPH *and other onlookers run to her*)

JOSEPH. What is it?

PAOLA. Nothing. Only Madame Blanchard helping herself to ten minutes or so of oblivion. Send all these people away, and fetch Barbette the blood-letter, from across the road.

     (JOSEPH *and the* CUSTOMERS *retire*)

PAOLA. Well, there you are. There you are, fast asleep. But this sleep is going to carry you to a shore you never imagined you would visit . . . How beautiful you look, my little enemy, beautiful and precise, as perfectly cut and finished as a key. What am I going to unlock with you, I wonder? Scandal? Disaster? We shall soon see. The moulding and notching of this beautiful key makes it all very promising; it will be a considerable scandal, an unprecedented disaster. I have here the golden key of Pandora's box. And it's just as you wanted it, Lucile; you wanted to unlock hatred and let it out.

     (BARBETTE *enters hurriedly*)

BARBETTE. The poor woman! What can I do?

PAOLA. You can help me to take a revenge. On her. A better
work of revenge than you ever did for me before. I'll pay you
double.

BARBETTE. A thorn in a facial nerve, shall it be? Or that drug
to make her come out in sores?

PAOLA. Certainly not. She's one of those high-minded souls
who become more beautiful with adversity. Is your house on
the Brignoles road still empty?

BARBETTE. Yes, it is. There are clean sheets on the bed.

PAOLA. You will have to soil them. How quiet, clear, and
innocent her sleep is. And what a scent floats out of her. It's
not like that with you and me, Barbette; what escapes from
us, when the sun has gone down, is the bitterness of the
world, which the trees drink in to their cost. What a beautiful
night it would be for men if there was nothing on earth except
the trees and this woman.

BARBETTE. What has she done to you?

PAOLA. She denounced us.

BARBETTE. Both of us?

PAOLA. All of us. From Cleopatra to Barbette, along with the
Queen of Sheba and the town clerk's wife.

BARBETTE. To the police?

PAOLA. To a man. She has told a man that women aren't all
angels.

BARBETTE. Shall I cut off her eyelashes? Shall I make her
grow a moustache?

PAOLA. You can take her in my carriage. Then lay her on the
bed. Undo her bodice, loosen her stockings, and let down her
hair. Lying dishevelled is a splendour she never knew with
her law-giving husband, her god the judge. So give it to her.
Flowers on the table, but the vase knocked over. Sandal-
wood at the bedside, but crushed under foot. The taste of
honey in her mouth, but running on to her chin. Charm her
senses before she feels her loathing for the bed.

BARBETTE. It would be dangerous to send a client in to her.

PAOLA. Nothing need happen; it's enough if she thinks it
happened.

BARBETTE. Who shall I say it was? An old man would be
amusing. An old tramp.

PAOLA. Not with her. No, it should be the most handsome
man possible, the best bred and the most subtly corrupting.

BARBETTE. Count Marcellus?

PAOLA. Count Marcellus. Here is his handkerchief. I took it
from him as I went past. Make sure that she has it in her
hand. Now I leave her to you. But arrange things so that when
she first wakes, before she sees herself, she feels she has had a
heavenly dream. Take this handkerchief, then. That's right,
keep good hold of it. It is woven with Ariadne's thread and
leads irrevocably to disaster.

CURTAIN

ACT II

MARCELLUS'S *house or apartment.*

(PAOLA. MARCELLUS)

MARCELLUS. Well, what's brought you here, so early in the morning? It isn't last year now.

PAOLA. This is your wedding morning.

MARCELLUS. Are you the bride?

PAOLA. No, I'm not here to be compensated. I mean a true marriage, Marcellus. One that you'll thank me for.

MARCELLUS. I doubt that. What true marriages do you know in this world?

PAOLA. I know a very interesting one. Vice with virtue.

MARCELLUS. Vice! You're talking like Mr. Justice Blanchard, and he talks like an old maid, and she talks like God. You can't expect a man to be Vice at eight o'clock in the morning. At that hour of the day Vice is essentially feminine.

PAOLA. I know you have a theory that men wake up each morning thoroughly newly born. Whatever they are at any other time, in the morning they're spotless children of the new day.

MARCELLUS. Yes, you might say that. Which is why you used to disturb me so last year, always insisting we should meet at dawn. You should know that when a man wakes he is always in the arms of his true wife, whoever is lying beside him. And it takes a certain time to forget her. You definitely used to arrive too early.

PAOLA. If you have a true wife it's cowardice, and the same is true of any man. He trusts himself to the arms of cowardice when he goes to sleep. A sleeping man is a sad sight for a woman who loves him. It's a sleep that rejects her altogether. You sleep without your desire, Marcellus, without your needs, and without your strength, like Lionel Blanchard sleeping without his decorations.

30

MARCELLUS. Without his decorations? I doubt that. But at any rate he sleeps with Madame Blanchard, which is what I find it hard to forgive him; and I mean to make him pay for it.

PAOLA. And if he isn't the only one, would he be so hard to forgive?

MARCELLUS. Your cynicism is losing quality, Paola. Cynicism, like modesty, should come straight from the heart.

PAOLA. Do you think I am jealous of Madame Blanchard?

MARCELLUS. I think you're jealous of innocent women in general. If you didn't know that, I'm telling you now. And I suggest you should be on your guard against it. You become very provincial whenever you're with them. You follow them about, and study them, as though purity were a secret which could be learnt. You look as though you were trying to catch up with the latest fashion; like someone anxious to copy a hat, or remember the details of a dress: to find the secret. The secret you will never know: how to caress a man without seeing him, how to see him without defining him: the secret of Lucrece, and of Madame Blanchard.

PAOLA. Choose better examples. I'm not reliable on the subject of Lucrece. But since nine o'clock last night Madame Blanchard doesn't come into your category at all.

MARCELLUS. That's a lie!

PAOLA. What vehemence!

MARCELLUS. Only what it would be if you told me you were an inexperienced girl again.

PAOLA. Even so, it's the truth. Madame Blanchard has fallen, as they say, prey to a seducer. It was at Barbette's house; Barbette saw everything.

MARCELLUS. Barbette is lying.

PAOLA. Men are so unsubtle. As soon as they see a woman they want, they think they can behave like a husband and demand proofs of fidelity. Well, here they are. Here is a comb that Barbette picked up. And here is the man's handkerchief.

MARCELLUS. Tell me his name!

PAOLA. This is where you shout 'Hell and damnation!' I know it's on the tip of your tongue.

MARCELLUS. Tell me his name!

PAOLA. I hesitate to do that. You wouldn't believe me.

MARCELLUS. I kept waking up in the night, and found myself really trembling with joy. There I lay, going through in my mind the time-table of Madame Blanchard's day, thinking out the best way to trap her. It was the first time in my life a conquest was also going to help me to have my revenge.

PAOLA. Are you sure it was only for revenge? From what I saw yesterday, it looked as if revenge was handing the affair over to something softer hearted. And I noticed that though she pretends to see some unpleasant crawling creature on anyone not strictly chaste, she could see no such thing on you. But I can.

MARCELLUS. Ever since that woman came here I've thought of nobody else. You know that. It was a great favour the law-courts did me when they sent her here. Before that I'd only seen virtue in women whose virtue was easy; I'd made the most of glimpses of truth among the lies, touches of grace in the graceless, and so forth. The man who forestalled me with her can have done it only by force.

PAOLA. Quite so. By a pure and simple outrage.

MARCELLUS. What's the name of this brute? He'll answer to me for it!

PAOLA. Don't hurt him too much. It's you, it's yourself.

MARCELLUS. That's a poor joke.

PAOLA. I'm not joking. Your face is the only one that Madame Blanchard can see just now. Her lips are tightly shut on your name and no other. A shadow, with the weight of your bones and flesh, has glided in between her and everything surrounding her, between her and her husband, and her old Marseilles dinner service, and her poodle, and God.

MARCELLUS. What exactly are you trying to tell me! Explain what you mean! Has she noticed me?

PAOLA. She loathes you. You're the first person she's ever hated, so it has all the energy of the first hatred the world ever knew. She has undoubtedly noticed you; she has marked you down for the rest of time.

MARCELLUS. Did Joseph tell her about my speech?

PAOLA (*slowly*).   Yesterday, at about seven o'clock, she fainted. She came to herself during the night, lying on Barbette's bed, half undressed and generally distraught. She learned from her hostess that a man had brought her there, had shut himself in with her, and the man was you.

MARCELLUS. Who invented this ridiculous story?

PAOLA. Revenge. Female vengeance.

MARCELLUS. How can she believe it?

PAOLA. Barbette has faked up a hundred women to seem like virgins in her time. For once, she had to do the opposite, and you can be sure she did it splendidly. And anyway, the victim was clutching your handkerchief. That's the tradition. I know my classics. And now thank me.

MARCELLUS. For giving away to my shadow what I was going to get for myself?

PAOLA.   Don't exaggerate. Your charms are on the decline. I took so much trouble to let you into my cousin Celestina's house on Saturday, and you couldn't even succeed with her.

MARCELLUS. Celestina doesn't prove anything. Celestina was perfectly willing, but she had some milk on the fire.

PAOLA. Well, it's now we shall see how much your reputation is worth, Marcellus my dear. Madame Blanchard is yours, if you want her. I know what she's like. She is purity itself, and purity, like sanctity, is imagination overflowing. Can't you see what power over her I've already given you?

MARCELLUS. Go on with your story. Where is she now? You were there at Barbette's house. You followed her there and spied on her. I know what you are: you like to see the evil you're doing.

PAOLA. And the good, too, if you remember?

MARCELLUS. What did she say?

PAOLA. She didn't say anything. She listened to everything Barbette told her, and said nothing. Barbette maintains that her clothes and her hair tidied themselves of their own accord. She didn't ever want to touch herself again, though she has since discovered that won't be easy. One of her knees

soon brushed against the other. The contact was awful to
her! And there are mirrors in her room at home. By now her
eyes will have met their own reflection.

MARCELLUS. So she has gone home?

PAOLA. She went off aimlessly into the dark, like a sleep-
walker, holding herself straight and stiff. She neither touched
the chapel wall she was passing, nor the dog which jumped
up to her. She leaned over the bridge without touching the
parapet: no expression in her eyes as she looked down at the
river. A white owl wheeled over her head. She looked up at
the owl; but nothing more came of it. And then suddenly she
weakened; she dared to touch a tree, a young, proud-looking
tree, with a round, smooth trunk, something between an
aspen and a lime.

MARCELLUS. The limes are in flower. You could have known
it by the scent.

PAOLA. Then it wasn't a lime. Any scent would have made her
fly for her life. The tree was breathing and whispering, with
a tenderness unusual in a tree. So she left it and went on.
She must have remembered that her husband was away, and
now she had reached home again. She stared up at the house
for a long time, and then she went in. I'll swear to you she
didn't touch the door. Midnight struck, just as she crossed
the threshold. She stopped dead. It was already the day after
her crime. The light was on in her room for a long while
afterwards. Poor woman! All the perfumes of Arabia
wouldn't sweeten a stain which in fact doesn't exist. So now,
Marcellus, to work. Her husband won't be back today. Now
it's your turn.

MARCELLUS. I'll go there. I don't think much of my chances.
But I'm in the mood to content myself with a scandal.

PAOLA. Your chances couldn't be better. Understand that.
She doesn't belong to her husband any more. She may refuse. But these women who don't hold with love, are all the
more likely to believe in possession – she belongs to you.
All you have to do is to take her back. You don't have to
compete with the judge any more: only with your own

ghost. So as long as you're not inferior to that, all is well.

MARCELLUS. Which is her room?

PAOLA. On the first floor: the door at the far end as you go through her husband's office. You're in riding breeches; that's wonderful. There's nothing so impressive as a good horseman climbing the stairs.

(*A bell rings. Pause. Enter a* MANSERVANT)

MARCELLUS. What is it?

SERVANT. There's a lady to see you, sir.

MARCELLUS. Who?

SERVANT. She wouldn't give a name, sir; I don't know her.

MARCELLUS. Is she wearing a veil?

SERVANT. No, sir; no veil.

PAOLA. Is she a nervous lady?

SERVANT. No, madam; the calmest that ever came here.

PAOLA. With clear grey eyes?

SERVANT. Yes, madam.

MARCELLUS. Ask her to come up.

(*Exit* MANSERVANT)

PAOLA. We've been forestalled, Marcellus. I'll go into your room.

MARCELLUS. That's no good to you. You won't be able to overhear anything at all from there.

PAOLA. It's been a tiring night. For the first time, you can let me use your room to sleep in. Here comes the unicorn. You'd better make sure, when she leaves, she's a less legendary animal.

(*She goes. Enter* LUCILE)

LUCILE. Are you Count Marcellus?

MARCELLUS. I am.

LUCILE. And since last night isn't it unbearable to be Count Marcellus?

MARCELLUS. It is. But the fact remains.

LUCILE. Wouldn't you give your life to be the Count Marcellus you were yesterday?

MARCELLUS. I gave more than that last night to be what I am today.

LUCILE. To have to face me like this?

MARCELLUS. To have to face you, above all people.

LUCILE. Did you look at yourself in the mirror this morning?

MARCELLUS. I can't stop looking at myself. I look so young and handsome and happy. Did you?

LUCILE. I looked only once. But I saw what I am, and what I have to do. Most clearly.

MARCELLUS. What I saw was someone who had taken his revenge, not on a hypocritical judge, but on my own too casual way of living. It was weighing me down with shoddy vulgarity. But one day I caught sight of something transcendant and inaccessible. I wanted it, no matter how. I got it. If you've come here, expecting to find me shattered with remorse, you'll be disappointed.

LUCILE. I'm not disappointed. I prayed for you to be as you are.

MARCELLUS. I don't know whether the woman you saw in the mirror told you to let justice and hatred loose on my tracks. But from now on I've got one aim in life, and one only. To stay as I am today. Never to touch any other form of nourishment. To go over and over in my mind an hour which no other man in the world has had. And to nourish my spirit, and my language, and my senses, with that memory, until the day I can surprise you a second time, and have the same pleasure again.

LUCILE. I see I was right to come here.

MARCELLUS. But you're not here at all! Don't you believe it for a moment! You're not the woman who's looking at me and talking like this. You are what you were last night: a body unconscious, but willing, with eyes which are seeing nothing but are wide open: a whispering voice, without a word being said. Why are you here? No more pretending!

Last night saw the end of the frozen automaton you used to be.

LUCILE. I came to see you.

MARCELLUS. And you do see me. You saw me yesterday, in your sleep. You recognized then the one who had been promised to you, though you kept your need of him even hidden from yourself. But when he was going away you clung to him.

LUCILE. I'm not clinging to you now.

MARCELLUS. But you will again. If not today, then tomorrow. You've understood that I was never in love before, but I am now.

LUCILE. Did you make these protestations to me when I couldn't hear them?

MARCELLUS. Yes, but you did hear them. And answered me with your body, clear promises, without the least shadow of doubt.

LUCILE. Have you a wife and children?

MARCELLUS. I have a wife. You, by one day.

LUCILE. She is my concern. I've heard people speak of a Countess Marcellus.

MARCELLUS. My mother. Until yesterday she had no cause to be proud of me.

LUCILE. What is she like?

MARCELLUS. On any ceremonial occasion, really beautiful. Particularly at marriages and funerals. A bit too dignified. A trifle opinionated.

LUCILE. Then she will forgive me what I am going to ask you. She will certainly understand . . .

MARCELLUS. You can ask me what you like, without worrying about anyone else.

LUCILE. I know. I have the right, and I mean to take it. But you don't seem to guess what I'm going to ask you.

MARCELLUS. Not yet. Looking at you makes it difficult to concentrate.

LUCILE. And yet it's so obvious. And I haven't any choice. And I don't hesitate to ask you. I know you to be a liar and a trickster, without either generosity or goodness of soul. But

I think you've got courage. If I'm wrong, correct me . . .
Don't come any nearer.

MARCELLUS. I didn't move. Even at this distance it's so good
to see my dear, blind wife with her eyes open at last.

LUCILE. There's honour, I suppose, even in lechery?

MARCELLUS. And to hear my dear, dumb wife speaking.

LUCILE. Then listen to her. For me, there has never been any
name but one for the union of a man with a woman. I have
been your wife. I am not one of those who, in my position,
would agree to say nothing and forget. An atrocious trick has
united me with you. It's impossible for me to be united to
anyone else. I don't think it's possible to loathe anyone more
than I loathe you. If I had to use your Christian name I
should vomit blood. If I touched you I should have to cry
out. But I can't see how it is possible to ignore the truth as it
is in the sight of God: because it was God you compelled to
be my witness last night. You have taken me, and poisoned
everything, even the things I love. Neither despair nor reason
can help me. Your crime has left me nothing to do except
give up the only respect I still have any right to, my own self-
respect. There's no other way to make myself clean again, and
so I have to accept it. I am bound to you; any other tie is
broken. My happiness has gone, my beloved husband has
been taken away; nothing is left to me except misery and a
loathsome husband.

MARCELLUS. Husband! That word's enough to glorify any
adjective you give it! Thank you.

LUCILE. Keep your thanks. I don't mean to follow this path
like a helpless lamb. I had a different husband yesterday, and
I want to find him again. He comes home at dawn tomorrow,
and I mean to find him as soon as he returns. I mean his wife
to receive him in total loyalty. Without reservation. Tomorrow morning he will knock at the door, but it must be
still possible for him to be her husband.

MARCELLUS. I defy him to be, and I defy you to be his wife.
You've been telling me yourself, since yesterday you're nobody's wife but mine.

LUCILE. I could be a widow.

MARCELLUS. My widow?

LUCILE. I know it would be easy to kill myself. But that's something I don't accept. I've done nothing to deserve death. I saw that when I went back to my home, where I thought everything would cover me with contempt. But everything thought well of me, and had compassion. Even my bed, my marriage-bed, welcomed me as naturally as the bed I slept in when I was little. Not one hour of the night, or of the dawn when it came, made me feel an outcast. If a single stone had told me to kill myself, I should have done so. But the stones told me to live. One growl from a dog would have destroyed me. But the dogs licked my face. But they made one condition: that your wickedness shouldn't leave any mark on me. I would have to transform it into a kind of collision with another period of time, and think of you as belonging to a past already vanished away. You must kill yourself; and then I may be able to speak of you without disgust. Give me your answer.

MARCELLUS. Let me first congratulate myself. I've reached the most beautiful moment of my career: receiving a visit from death, like the engravings of death calling Don Juan to account for all his crimes.

LUCILE. I'm not interested in your crimes. I cling to your death like a child to its mother. It's the only thing that can lead me back to life.

MARCELLUS. I am your husband, Lucile.

LUCILE. I have a black dress. I will wear it tomorrow. Give me your answer.

MARCELLUS. Why this contempt? You know very well what answer I'm going to give.

LUCILE. No, I'm not entirely sure of it. I've been watching you since I came here. Until last night I thought I knew you. But I see now, this was not true. You're as far away from death as a condemned man is from the guillotine. A pity for you. You will have to make the journey on foot.

MARCELLUS. Willingly, but the journey begins with you.

LUCILE. Let me go!

MARCELLUS. Never again. You're not free of your marriage yet. You still belong to me. And while that is so, even if only for a few hours more, I have the right to ask everything I want from you.

LUCILE. Oh, God, he's a coward!

MARCELLUS. You're my wife! You've said so. Don't think I'm content with a wedding night which you weren't even aware of. I know what you are myself, caressing and yielding, loving and giving. But you don't know it yet. I suggest that it's time you did. It's beautiful to see virtue arguing with love.

LUCILE. I hate you!

MARCELLUS. You don't hate me. A woman never confesses the truth with her mouth, or even thinks it in her head; it has to be fetched up out of her guts. Which is what I've done.

LUCILE. You've got to die! You've got to die!

MARCELLUS. All right, I'll die. Do you think I'm afraid to do it? I've found you, and I can vanish. Say the word, and I disappear. Any day or hour you like. I give you my word. But only on condition that I can have you in my arms one more time.

LUCILE. I don't hear you.

MARCELLUS. You do hear me, but I'll say it again. If you'll be my wife, just once again, on my honour, I'll kill myself. I'll kill myself immediately afterwards. Do you hear me this time?

LUCILE. No.

MARCELLUS. Your marriage vows call you. Lie down!

ARMAND (*offstage*). Let her alone, Marcellus.

(*Enter* ARMAND)

MARCELLUS. What do you want here?

ARMAND. What I couldn't be sure I should find. Something like my honour. But fortune favours me. Don't go, madam. You can leave with me presently.

MARCELLUS. Get out of this house.

ARMAND. No. I'm not suggesting the house is mine. But they tell me that my wife used to come here every morning last year. So I have the right to come here one morning this year. One single morning. And I've come at the time she used to come. You won't see me here again.

MARCELLUS. You're late, as a matter of fact.

ARMAND. I was late to start with, I agree. I had come here because of my wife. I was as late as trusting husbands always are when they've been deceived. A year late, or a month, it's all the same. But I've been here some few minutes – the door was on the latch, and I made my way up – I've heard all that you've been saying; and I get the impression that I'm right on time.

LUCILE. Let us go. I must ask you to take me away.

ARMAND. Do what I tell you. Stay here, while I have my say, and say as little as you did in the café yesterday. Your silence today will give me back what your silence took away then. And more.

MARCELLUS. I order you to leave!

ARMAND. I don't take orders from you, though I understand your feelings. I expect it seems odd to you to see a man in your house. Not at all as it should be. He doesn't sit down and look at your pictures, with a beating heart, cooing like a dove. Intolerable. He knows what he's here for. And that's disturbing. You're afraid, aren't you?

MARCELLUS. You may as well know, you're not much good at taking a strong line.

ARMAND. I know I'm not. I'm no good at anything, either as a husband or a friend. That's the way it is. The station in life that I've been called to isn't very seductive. In fact nothing on earth is very seductive, except a seducer.

MARCELLUS. Thanks, and now go.

ARMAND. It wasn't a compliment. A seducer never seduces anybody. He's the poor wretch that other men make use of, to rid themselves of women who're too silly or wanton or over-demanding. You're the victim, my poor chap. Take Paola, for instance . . .

MARCELLUS. Paola has nothing to do with this argument.
Paola is a friend of mine, that's all.

ARMAND. You don't really understand anything, Marcellus!
You treat today as though it were like every other day. But
as soon as I opened my window I could see that today is a day
of reckoning. The sky is clear blue, but an invisible line cuts
sheer across it: you can tell at once it's a judgement sky. You
should have opened your window this morning, and looked
at the line in the sky. It would have encouraged you to make
up your accounts. It would also have prompted you to be
honest, and not to say 'Paola is a friend, and that's all'. It's
funny how a betrayed husband can't stop talking about his
wife.

MARCELLUS. It's funny how husbands who think they're betrayed are more crass than those who really are.

ARMAND. I'm intelligent. I'm betrayed all right. Poor Paola.
She's as promiscuous as she can be, but she didn't think of
destroying the evidence. She burnt all the letters, never accepted a portrait, removed every identifying mark from the
gifts she was given. When you gave her roses, she would even
add one or two from our garden, to disguise where they came
from. But she couldn't confuse my memory. As though everything my unconscious thought wrote on my memory is being
made visible in the light of unhappiness. You've arrived at
the day of reckoning, Marcellus. No denying that Paola used
to come here. She came twenty times, a hundred times. She
knew this room intimately. She used to light these lamps, or
turn them low; she knew these chairs and this sofa well. If I
called out 'Paola!' she would come running in herself. Shall
I?

MARCELLUS. You've gone mad.

ARMAND. Don't worry. I won't call her. I shall never call
Paola again. The scent has led me to you and not to her. You
are the one I have to deal with, but not because of Paola.

MARCELLUS. You mean, because of Madame Blanchard.

ARMAND. Precisely. I am happy, Marcellus. Last night I believed that I was thinking of Paola. There's no doubt my

dreams and the pattern of my thoughts began with her, with despair and disgust, but now they were all the time turning towards someone else. Lying awake, I found myself turning from hatred and jealousy towards happiness. To the knowledge that Madame Blanchard was alive and breathing.

MARCELLUS. Madame Blanchard is alive, certainly; and she belongs to me.

ARMAND. We shall see where she belongs. But first of all we both have to kneel down before her, my dear Marcellus. Thanks to her, our poor town has taken a turn for the better. Aix was sadly lacking in greatness and heroism. Madame Blanchard hasn't only brought grace and simple upright living to Aix; she has changed us all, Marcellus, changed you, the untroubled libertine, and me, the untroubled honest husband, and shone a light which seems to have become very like the light of death. All blood and sun! Your shoddiness, and my ingenuousness, are both made bright with death, dear Marcellus. We've no more time to lose. I came here to challenge you, because of Paola, but I found I'd forgotten Paola before I got to your door, and then I overheard your conversation with Madame Blanchard. So now, if you don't mind, it will be because of Madame Blanchard.

MARCELLUS. Just as you like, you ass; I'm entirely at your service. It can be because of every woman who ever came into this house, if that's what you want.

ARMAND. It all comes to the same thing. Anyway, I explain myself badly; your opinion isn't important. If Madame Blanchard agrees, it shall be because of her.

MARCELLUS. And as you well know, since you were spying on us, that's exactly what she wants.

ARMAND. Be quiet . . . I overheard what you said, madam, and I entirely agree. This man broke into your life by a crime, and the only way to rid your life of him may very well be to rid him of his own. With your permission, I'm going to fight him. He has laid my life in ruins as well. It won't be difficult to see this duel as a judgement of God. What do you say? Are you willing to accept me?

LUCILE. *He* won't be willing. He's a coward.

MARCELLUS. You can send your seconds to me. I shall be at home all the evening.

ARMAND. We can't wait until this evening. Madame Blanchard has suffered too long already. Our seconds are waiting for us in St. Mary's fields, with the pistols: I took leave to prepare them, all four of them, yours and mine. None of them turned a hair. They all knew about your affair with Paola. Yours are young Montbaran and your cousin.

MARCELLUS. All right. We'll get little Montbaran to step out the thirty paces. He's got the shortest legs.

ARMAND. There, you see, madam, he isn't a coward. He's vain; vain in a minor sort of way; his blood circulates without a heart. He knows my skill with a pistol, and he's a poor shot himself. He has a very estimable mother. He has a governess who loves him, and dogs that worship him. But he isn't a coward. Are you willing to accept me?

LUCILE (*with a nod*). Yes.

MARCELLUS. Downstairs we go, then, you gallant defender! One thing I'll tell you to put you in good form: the favours of Paola at her most lively are nothing compared with Madame Blanchard's when she's unconscious!

ARMAND. You're taking leave of her now. Is that all you have to say to her?

MARCELLUS. That's all. If she hadn't accepted you, I should probably have told her something else, something which might have been worth at least another kiss to me, and the most grateful kiss of them all. But she'll never hear it now, whether I live or die. Neither will you.

ARMAND. Wait until we have gone, madam, and then go home. You will get news there whether we've lost or won.

LUCILE. Come back again.

ARMAND. Good-bye, madam. Thank you. For today as well as for yesterday.

(*Exeunt* ARMAND *and* MARCELLUS. *Enter* PAOLA)

PAOLA. A hard moment for you, Lucile, but here is a friend.

LUCILE. I might have known you wouldn't be far away.

PAOLA. A friend, I promise you. That's not blasphemy. To every new world a new language. And a friend doesn't seem to you now someone to gossip with about clothes and running a house; it means someone to be beside you in this new life of yours, being a woman in a world of men, an accomplice, a twin spirit, a go-between; and all these things I can be.

LUCILE. I knew it! This terrible nightmare is your doing!

PAOLA. What terrible nightmare? The day was bound to come when you would have to give up performing your unconvincing dance of virginity. Love has taken you unaware, while you were asleep, as it probably took Eve unaware in the garden. What a happy thing it would be for us if it were always like that, a great economy of feeling and effort.

LUCILE. Why did you drug me, Paola? Why were you so cowardly?

PAOLA. Paola! At last you've called me by my christian name! The barriers are down!

LUCILE. Be quiet. You are waiting for a man's death, and you are talking.

PAOLA. It's quite proper. People usually talk while they're sitting up with the dead. Look how sisters-in-law who don't like each other quite shamelessly start quarrelling under their breath while they watch by the dying bedside. That's why people in our families die, that the real causes of argument can be brought out into the light of death.

LUCILE. And of hatred, too: don't you think?

PAOLA. Hatred doesn't cure anything, Lucile. You'll come to take a serener, wiser view of this accident presently. And that's just why I came to help you. To you it seems a monstrous wrong, but possible to remedy. Both of those ideas are false. There's no remedy for what happened to you, but it doesn't matter. Love leaves no trace, Lucile. When a woman gets tired of something, it simply isn't there. I sometimes pass men in the street who convey nothing at all to me, who don't touch my imagination, or have any masculine appeal for me whatsoever. You can be sure they were lovers of mine in the past.

LUCILE. Someone rang! Someone is here! They must be back!

PAOLA. No, not they. I do wish you would learn to know them. They take themselves too seriously to hurry matters. First of all they have to give a dignified bow to the seconds. And at least one of them has to take off his cravat, a most important matter for a man, and the doctor drops his spectacles in the long grass and has to look for them. Even the carriage horses which took them there have a particular slow pace which is called the duelling trot.

LUCILE. You're talking so much, Paola. You're not at ease in your mind. And when someone like you, who has all the graces and all the vices, launches such an attack on someone like me, the only reason there can be for it is that you're afraid.

PAOLA. Afraid of you?

LUCILE. No, not of me – yourself. For I know you despise yourself at this moment. Face to face with me, you feel small and ashamed that you can't stop being ironical and spiteful when I'm suffering.

PAOLA. You're in a melodrama, and I'm in real life. There's a fundamental discord there.

LUCILE. Don't try to drag me over to your side of life. Here, at my own level of unhappiness, I can count on all the resources of God, from miracles to death. I stand beside those who found help for their suffering in turning away from this corrupt world, and confiding instead in a world where everything is possible. You won't bring me down to yours.

PAOLA. It's rather presumptuous, don't you think, over an accident as slight and venial as yours is, to call out for help to the saints and martyrs?

LUCILE. One calls on whoever will reply. When I called, all those women answered who know that what has been done can be redeemed. Those who were stripped naked in front of the crowd, and yet made a cloak out of their nakedness and crossed the town by the main streets. Those whose nails were torn off, and the blood on their fingers became heavenly nails, and they went on with their work. Or those who were stretched over a fire, and the bars of the grid-iron branded heavenly music on their bodies, and they rose up singing. They have all reassured me that presently I shall return home, calm and unaltered. I shall lie on my bed tonight as untouched as I was before. The price of this is Marcellus's death, but since it was God who faced me with this dilemma, it is God who is giving him his death, and not I. And now God is giving you your answer. Armand has come back.

(*Enter the* MANSERVANT)

SERVANT. Mr. Justice Blanchard is downstairs, madam.

LUCILE. Heavens!

PAOLA. What does he want?

SERVANT. He heard that Madame Blanchard was here. He's waiting for her.

PAOLA. A pause in the high drama, while we indulge in a scene of domestic comedy.

LUCILE. Did you send for him?

PAOLA. No, but I expected him, and it's your own fault he has come. Yesterday, in the café, you inconsiderately betrayed all the women in the world, and roused all the men to a hue-and-cry. Today, from one side of the world to the other, the men are going to arrive too soon, leave too late, guess correctly, intercept the incriminating letter and make themselves thoroughly insupportable. God has been pipped at the post by your husband. You can't blame anybody except yourself. What will you decide to do?

LUCILE. I don't want him to see me! I don't want anyone to see me, until Armand has come back.

PAOLA. It doesn't matter so much if your husband sees you. He's not going to notice that your lips are a little riper, and your eyes the faintest degree larger; no husband would. What matters is that you will see him, and see him with the eyes of a woman who has been unfaithful to him for the

first time; after years of being blind to him you are going to
see him as he really is. That's what is terrifying you, and I can
understand it. And that's my revenge, Lucile. You will see
him in his total reality. Yesterday he was simple, generous,
and good. What is he going to be when he comes in through
that door? You will never have seen a man you knew less
about.

LUCILE. Very well. Let him come in. He can know everything.

PAOLA. Don't be idiotic, and do make some effort to understand me. However much I may hate a woman, she still ranks
higher with me than any man does, and you and I are going
to be great friends yet. By wrestling naked together, as we
have since yesterday, we've gained an understanding which
has certain duties. Take this staircase here, it leads down to
the street. Your husband knows nothing. I shall tell him that
you came here out of friendship for me, to help me through
an ordeal, and that you've already left again. I'll keep him
here long enough to give you time to get quietly home.

LUCILE. Good-bye.

PAOLA. Au revoir, Lucile, until this evening when we shall sit
like sisters eating our ices under the lime trees, as though
nothing had happened.

LUCILE. Never!

PAOLA. Oh yes, Lucile.

LUCILE. I can never be one of your kind. Your devilish tricks
are no use. Hissing like a snake isn't going to do you any
good.

(*Exit* LUCILE)

PAOLA (*slowly, taking pleasure in hissing the words*). Oh yes,
Lucile, it is, yes, it is!

CURTAIN

ACT III

MR. JUSTICE BLANCHARD'S *house. His private office, which leads to his room, and* LUCILE'S. *Busts of Cujas and Lycurgus.*

(LIONEL BLANCHARD. *The* CLERK *of the* COURT)

BLANCHARD (*at his table*). Give me the interrogations in the Thomasse case. Cavaillon tells me that it's going to be heard this afternoon.

CLERK. I'll fetch them for you, sir.

BLANCHARD. Did no one tell you I was back?

CLERK. I have just seen Madame Blanchard on the stairs. She went past without speaking to me.

BLANCHARD. You must have made a mistake. Madame Blanchard isn't here.

CLERK. Then you'll find her double in her room, sir. I saw her go in.

(*Exit the* CLERK. BLANCHARD *hesitates, rises, and knocks at* LUCILE'S *door*)

BLANCHARD. Are you there, Lucile? . . . Lucile! Lucile!

(*He hears the* CLERK *coming back, and returns to his table*)

CLERK. Thomasse is still protesting that he's not guilty, sir, and goes on stuffing himself with olives.

BLANCHARD. So the Investigation can't get him to confess, before the trial begins, that he killed his wife?

CLERK. Not yet. They're going to stop the supply of olives at noon today.

BLANCHARD. The Investigation has already, successively and quite uselessly, in the order in which he most enjoys them, deprived him of artichokes, tomatoes, and pimentoes. As a form of torture, it seems less effective than the thumbscrew. The statement of the first witnesses?

49

CLERK. I'll fetch them for you, sir.

(*He goes out.* BLANCHARD *rises and knocks at* LUCILE'S *door*)

BLANCHARD. Lucile! It is I, Lionel! I was called back home, by express message. Are you there? You are there! I can hear you. Open the door, dearest . . . Why is this? You've locked yourself in! Please, my dear, open the door. Even if you're busy writing a letter to slip into my hand before the trial, one of your sweet letters wishing me good luck in my speech to the court.

(*As the* CLERK *returns,* BLANCHARD *goes back to his desk and signs the papers which the* CLERK *brings him*)

CLERK. All the same, sir, this depriving him of things: it was successful in the Tourmaire case. Tourmaire had killed his father, you may remember, and wouldn't confess it. Depriving him of cabbage salad got the most hair-raising details out of him. He heated hairpins in the fire, you remember, and when they were white hot . . .

BLANCHARD. What was the exact date he was committed?

CLERK. I'll fetch it for you, sir.

BLANCHARD. When I ring for you. I have some work to do.

(*The* CLERK *goes out. A* SERVANT *has brought in some flowers which he puts down on a table.* BLANCHARD *goes back to* LUCILE'S *door*)

BLANCHARD. Lucile, are you ill? Do answer me. Say something! If you don't open the door, Lucile, I shall force it!

(*The door opens. Enter* LUCILE)

BLANCHARD. Well, at last, Lucile!

LUCILE. Lionel, why have you come back so soon?

BLANCHARD. So soon!

LUCILE. Why did you knock? Why did you make me open the door?

BLANCHARD. I thought you must have fainted, Lucile dear. I didn't know what to think.

LUCILE. You didn't know what to think! What do you think now?

BLANCHARD. I breathe again. I see my wife, my adorable wife again, and I've brought her some flowers.

LUCILE. Flowers! Armand wasn't so blind.

BLANCHARD. You mustn't let the duel upset you. Paola warned me about it, and I've sent the mounted police to stop them fighting.

LUCILE. Will they get there in time?

BLANCHARD. They've gone at a gallop. It's worth it if they can save Armand's life. Marcellus is a good shot.

LUCILE. And surely a good target, as well?

BLANCHARD. I hope you weren't displeased that I went to his house to look for you? You'll have to forgive me. When I got back I couldn't stand being in the house without you. What vase shall we have the flowers in? The Meissen?

LUCILE. What was the house like without me?

BLANCHARD. Full of you, just as it is now, even though you weren't there. You're making strawberry jam, aren't you? An incredible scent; I love it. If the Investigation deprives me of it I shall publicly confess to loving you . . . I sat down at this desk, and looked at the pens and the sharpened pencils you had put ready for me, and felt loved and waited for. I took up this new pen, blessed you for remembering it was my favourite kind, and corrected my indictment. By far the most fascinating one of my career: this Thomasse case: he killed his wife. It's a pity that the world's first murder was a man killing a man; it means I can't refer to it in my speech. But my reference to the first woman ever killed by a husband, Sara her name was, is very fine; it ought to make a great impression on the court, I think. I rehearsed the whole speech in front of the mirror. But you weren't there, as you've always been before, to help me with your opinion. It was no use. My little Lucile hadn't slipped into the robes of Justice, to help me in the pursuit of crime. So I had to go and find you.

LUCILE. And have you found me now?

BLANCHARD. Indeed I have.

LUCILE. And you'll take me in your arms? Will you kiss me?

BLANCHARD. With the tenderest recognition that a husband and magistrate responsible for the Thomasse case has ever felt.

LUCILE. Can you see me quite clearly?

BLANCHARD. Wonderfully.

LUCILE. Let me go.

BLANCHARD. I'm sorry.

LUCILE. Lionel, I've changed since yesterday. Don't you see?

BLANCHARD. Your dress, you mean? Or altered in looks? I don't see any difference.

LUCILE. My hair, my dress, my mouth. Surely you see?

BLANCHARD. Your mouth? What are you talking about? Tell me what to look for.

LUCILE. It's so clear, so obvious. And you can't see.

BLANCHARD. Lucile, you're raving! What has happened to you? What were you doing yesterday?

LUCILE. What were you doing yesterday, Lionel, at eight o'clock?

BLANCHARD. Oh, good heavens, now I understand! You've been feeling jealous! Well, that's very gratifying; and in answer to the counsel for the prosecution, my darling wife, yesterday at eight o'clock, on the twenty-ninth of July, I was dining at Cavaillon with Counsellor Provencheres. At that precise moment he was opening a bottle of Château-Châlon which he gets direct from the Scee family themselves; he's related to them by marriage. It's a 'vin de paille', as you probably know, rather like Tokay, the parent vine was brought from Hungary by an abbess, who travelled with it hidden in her sleeve. It's a strong wine, but dry. We drank your health in it.

LUCILE. And you didn't find a scorpion at the bottom of the bottle?

BLANCHARD. Not at all. And the Strasbourg paté was remarkably free from earwigs and centipedes.

LUCILE. Then you were no clearer-sighted yesterday than you

are today. Lionel, listen; don't ask any questions, just do what
I tell you. Go away, leave at once! I beg you to. Your carriage
is still harnessed. Come back tomorrow at the time you
meant to come. Everything will be all right again tomorrow.

BLANCHARD. But what's the matter? You've changed, you
say! But I'm the one you are looking at as though I'm not the
same person any longer.

LUCILE. You will be tomorrow! Please go.

BLANCHARD. Lucile, my dear, I haven't been able to take you
with me up to the present. I've had to do all the accumula-
tion of work which my predecessors so obligingly left to be
done. Don't blame me for that; from now on you won't ever
have to be parted from me. I've bought a new carriage which
I was keeping as a surprise for you. It's got a special chest for
carrying cold meals, and a canteen of folding forks and col-
lapsible cups, with our monogram on. I've ordered you a new
carriage cape from Grenoble, because the wind is very keen
on the moors; and the field glasses you've always wanted, so
that you can follow the birds up into the sky, and pick out
any ghosts that may be wandering about in the castle ruins as
we go past. But there's a point I must make clear to you. The
success of a man's career is based, more than anything else,
on a woman's even temper and reliability. The foundation of
every successful enterprise a man undertakes, the root of
every fruitful career, is a woman who doesn't change, in
looks, or gesture, or voice. As one of my Roman predecessors so wisely said: *Ab una uxore unus vir. Una* to be
understood in the sense of 'uniformity', and *unus* in its sense
of 'uniqueness'. A unique man will always be found to have
an equable wife; and the same thing applies to men of talent
and brilliance, and, as in my own case, Lucile, of justice. I
lead a full, rich, and useful life because I don't have to nego-
tiate all the complicated lock-gates of temperament, and un-
certainties of the heart. This is the first time that I've looked
at you and seen a face I don't quite recognize . . . Has my
cravat come loose? What's wrong with it? . . . No! You
shall not go back to your room! I forbid you to!

LUCILE. Lionel, please! Let me alone, at least until we've had news of the duel!

LIONEL. You've got this duel on the brain. I can promise you, there won't be any duel. By the time they've decided which of the seconds shall pace out the distance, and long before the duellists have had time to take off their coats and untie their cravats, my police will have caught up with them. Sit down here beside me.

LUCILE. Then I must ask one question, Lionel.

LIONEL. When I've revised my indictment. I'll read it to you. Concentrate; you can be as critical as you like.

LUCILE. Lionel, it's a sort of question like a flash of lightning. If the mind doesn't answer it with the same speed, it can't be asked again. It is over for ever.

LIONEL. It isn't exactly a magistrate's *forte* to reply to flashes of lightning.

LUCILE. But suppose, early in my life, I'd had another husband, and was now a widow. You find that out. Would you take me back again? Would you marry me again?

LIONEL. Stop all this childish nonsense. If another man had touched my wife, whether the calendar went forwards or backwards, I wouldn't see her again as long as I lived.

LUCILE. Remembering she had been unconscious, Lionel, lifeless and unconscious.

LIONEL. The flesh is never unconscious.

LUCILE. The flesh! How can you use that terrible word to me? To say I have flesh!

LIONEL. You force me to. There are a thousand different ways of talking of the spirit, but the flesh is the flesh, even when it's yours. If a man had touched my wife, I should never touch her or speak to her again for the rest of my life.

LUCILE. Then, good-bye . . .

LIONEL. But what has happened? What are you trying to tell me?

LUCILE. What has happened is that you'll never touch me again. You'll never speak another word to me.

LIONEL. A man has dared to lay hands on you?

LUCILE. He has dared to marry me.

LIONEL. Stop using that ridiculous word! A man has touched you!

LUCILE. My word is the right word. Why did you come back so soon, Lionel? Everything good and innocent was rallying to help me. By coming home so soon, you've spoilt it all.

LIONEL. It's Marcellus! That's why you went to his house.

LUCILE. He drugged me last night, and carried me to one of his houses. I woke up, and Marcellus had gone.

LIONEL. Swear to me, swear that's true.

LUCILE. I didn't even see him. The reason I went to his house this morning . . .

LIONEL. Was to give this crime a face and a voice, to give him eyes to see you with!

LUCILE. Was to ask him to kill himself. And almost at the same moment Armand came to challenge him because of Paola. And now I'm waiting.

LIONEL. And you've even left it to someone other than me to avenge your honour.

LUCILE. I still keep my honour; it's the only thing that's not destroyed in me.

LIONEL. And you dare to call this degrading incident your second marriage!

LUCILE. It's the only way I could purify it. You, too! You, too!

LIONEL. You dare to say they were a husband's kisses that he gave you!

LUCILE. Oh, Lionel, do believe me, listen to me.

LIONEL. So you insist on calling yourself his wife until he's dead!

LUCILE. There may be only a minute to wait, only two minutes.

LIONEL. It won't be many more, whatever happens. (*He takes pistols from a drawer.*)

LUCILE. Lionel, Lionel dear!

(BLANCHARD *goes, bumping into the* CLERK)

CLERK. M. Blanchard, sir! Sir!

LUCILE. What do you want him for?

CLERK. Madam, the most important exhibit in the Thomasse case has disappeared out of the cupboard!

The phial of poison. I put it there yesterday evening.

LUCILE. You'd better hurry and find it. Go and look for it quickly!

(*The* CLERK *goes. Enter* ARMAND)

ARMAND. Good-bye, Lucile.

LUCILE. He's dead!

ARMAND. He's dying. I managed to avoid the police. I wanted to see you again before they arrested me.

LUCILE. He's dead!

ARMAND. He was condemned to die. God had stricken him with the malady which he gives to anyone he means to lose: made him slow.

LUCILE. Oh, Armand, it's too late.

ARMAND. I came here at a gallop. But I know your husband's coach has been quicker, and quicker than death, as well.

LUCILE. Yes. He's home.

ARMAND. But Marcellus has gone. The only thing that matters.

LUCILE (*after a pause*). Armand, are you sure of that?

ARMAND. So far as I feel I'm an avenger and not a murderer, yes.

LUCILE. Forgive me, Armand. But I think I have been wrong.

ARMAND. Wrong to be true to yourself?

LUCILE. To have had so much pride. Why should I have told Marcellus I was his wife? To have called it a marriage, instead of quite simply a great misfortune. Why wasn't I content to be the dishonoured wife with a loving, unhappy husband?

ARMAND. You still can be. The husband and the unhappiness are both still there.

LUCILE. That's just what I don't know, Armand. That's what is so frightening. The man I've just seen isn't the husband I thought he was yesterday. I've seen a man I never saw before, someone I never loved.

ARMAND. In a moment of shock a man can't always find the right mask to wear, to face the disaster. The mask of the outraged husband was in easy reach, and he took it. Give him time to put it down and you'll see his real face again.

LUCILE. All my life I won't forget the other. Oh, Armand, it's dreadful to think that if you take a man's wife away from him, he is changed from someone just and good and generous, into an egotistical bully. But that's what I've seen with my own eyes. His wonderful cloak of virtue, which he was so proud of, as I was, too, has fallen suddenly into rags. Everything he says sounds like hypocrisy and wrong-thinking, even though he is using words like honour and justice and the family. He quoted Latin as if he had lifted up a gravestone. Even the scent of the lotion on his chin, which I chose for him, and the cloth his suit is made of, which I also chose, were as alien and hostile to me as he was.

ARMAND (*after a pause*). Why are you telling me these things which you should only tell yourself?

LUCILE. So that you can reassure me. Oh, Armand, tell me what a man is, drive away this nightmare, and I'll believe you.

ARMAND. What a man is? From what I know of myself, all I can say is that he's neither complicated nor unique.

LUCILE. But generous and strong, isn't that so?

ARMAND. Gullible and unreal. He believes, first of all, if he's modest, that the world belongs to him completely. Then, if he's intelligent, he believes that woman belongs to him, and love belongs to him. Then, when his hope in life has given place to the pleasures of living, he groans away the night in silence, and weeps with a dry eye.

LUCILE. Is that everything?

ARMAND. Everything up to yesterday.

LUCILE. Go on. What is he today?

ARMAND. Today he has killed. The harmless one has killed: he is going to prison for murder. He has destroyed his life. He has seen you. He is happy.

LUCILE. Thank you. Lionel can come back. Good-bye.

(*Enter* PAOLA, *followed by* BARBETTE)

PAOLA. What's more, a man is pretentious, if he's one of the simple sort. Weak and feeble, if he's one of the passionate sort. And if he's timid, he gambles with destiny like a madman. And by that, I mean you.

ARMAND. Who have you brought here? Who is this woman?

PAOLA. She is splendid, isn't she? In every way like the destiny I mentioned.

ARMAND. What have you come here for?

PAOLA. To listen to you, amongst other things. It was well worth the trouble. I'm sure that martyrs have never mutually crowned each other with such laurels before. You may think you're defying death, but you're screaming love at each other like a pair of cats. I've come to avenge Marcellus, and it won't be difficult.

ARMAND. Leave Marcellus to his death, where you put him.

PAOLA. Don't quibble. You're the murderers. She killed him. You killed him. You, out of vanity. She, by thinking she was virtuous. You, by the honour of a gentleman. Both of you by chasing after tragedy when you're really deep in farce. But you won't be able to look at each other when I've said what I have to say to her.

ARMAND. Get away from here, or I'll take you away, whether you like it or not.

PAOLA. This woman is a criminal, Armand. If it hadn't been for her, you would still be happy with me, proud of me and rightly so. She understood nothing. She denounced me, without seeing that it was only her denunciation that made me guilty. My life took many different shapes, but not one of them encroached on the others. I wasn't like her; no woman is. She makes a sordid hotch-potch of her body and her sentimentality. Half like a schoolgirl, and half like a witch stirring you, and her husband, and Marcellus, all up together in one cauldron. I loved you yesterday, Armand. You were dearer to me than anyone in the world. If I've had lovers, they were outside our territory, nothing to do with the affection we had for each other. And we're all like that, except Lucile, who hasn't got our gift of forgetting, can't manage our transmigration of soul. I've always loved you completely and devotedly, with the whole of my being which belonged to you.

LUCILE. Everything this woman says is untrue. It isn't because I denounced her to you that she hates me but because I denounced her to herself. She thinks her loose-living is fine-spirited. She thinks every wicked affair she had was the fine flower of youth and beauty. And as she got older she would have become more and more sure of it. Her vicious past would have seemed correct and dignified. But my voice has changed all this into a waste of weeds and filth, and execration.

PAOLA. Alas, I have to disappoint you, dear Lucile. I'm handing my past over to you. You belong now to the regiment of women you refuse to acknowledge. You refuse to acknowledge yourself, now, and that's my revenge. This change in you, which so delights Armand, this languor, this passion, this slow, but very successful, alteration from the prudish magistrate's wife to the frightened woman obsessed by her predicament, has been brought about by no one but yourself. Listen to this, Armand. It's true there was a rape last night on the Brignoles road, but it wasn't Marcellus who was responsible . . .

LUCILE. Oh, heaven, protect me!

PAOLA. The responsible one is alive. Is there at this moment. Isn't that so, Barbette?

LUCILE. This woman is Barbette?

PAOLA. She is here to help you. Today even more than yesterday. And her moment has come. Come here, Barbette; and not as though you were falsehood, when in fact you're truth itself. She is here with the truth for you, and a truth which is going to horrify you.

ARMAND. Paola!

PAOLA. It isn't that Marcellus invited some friends to a drunken orgy, nor that a tramp saw an open window and an unconscious woman, and made the most of it. My revenges aren't so commonplace, Armand my darling. You're going to fall on my neck and bless me for this. But Madame Blanchard will be less relieved. She has a suspicion already that her dignity and respectability are escaping her: that she isn't Marcellus's widow after all; that this soft, guilty, pulsating body is hers by nature. Because Marcellus hasn't held her in his arms. Barbette is a witness to that. There was no assault last night. This morning she is just as she was yesterday, when she sat eating her strawberry ice, a narrow-minded woman, quite intact, who has never been touched by the hands or lips of anyone, except the honourable husband.

LUCILE. And Marcellus held his tongue. God, pity me!

PAOLA. Your hands are shaking, Lucile. And it isn't just the shame of looking ridiculous. What a disaster it is to lie down a martyr and rise a virgin! You are beginning to feel you have lost the only reason you had for believing in yourself, and you can't bear it.

ARMAND. What is it, Lucile?

LUCILE. Go away! Leave me alone, all of you!

ARMAND. I don't understand.

PAOLA. You will understand tomorrow. Men always understand – tomorrow. There you have the true scandalous story, Lucile. The rape last night was the work of Madame Blanchard herself. A case, you might say, of purity destroying itself. She boasted that she could tell immediately who was sinning, and how and when; but she couldn't recognize her own purity, couldn't tell, after all, that she hadn't been kissed and loved. She believed everything she was told, believed she moaned with joy, believed she held Marcellus back by his arm and his thigh. Sad for her that it's only a shadow.

LUCILE (*to* BARBETTE). Is this true, what this woman says?

BARBETTE. Yes, madam.

LUCILE. Nobody touched me but you?

BARBETTE. No, madam.

LUCILE. And the mark on my arm?

BARBETTE. I bit you, madam. Quite gently. Your flesh is tender. And the mark above your knee . . .

LUCILE. Did Count Marcellus not come in for a moment, or even see me? How did the hankerchief come to be in my hand?

BARBETTE. Madam put it there.

PAOLA. And brought it back again. And that's the end of that little interlude. And here we are, face to face again, as we were on the café terrace. I can only say again what I was saying then . . .

ARMAND. Come away with me, at once.

PAOLA (*losing control*). I have a mission. I'm going to finish it. (*To* LUCILE.) When you see a friend going off to visit her lover, you will give her your hand, and when she's returning, you'll smile at her; you'll talk and laugh with the deceived, indulgent husband. You will make quite sure that what you do won't lead a man into making believe he sees things as they are, and perhaps committing a crime. You can't say now that I'm only pleading my own cause . . . I think I heard your husband's carriage. Good-bye. A dead man is waiting for me, and a policeman is waiting for Armand, and neither of them, as we know, care to be kept waiting.

    (LIONEL *appears, running up the stairs*)

LUCILE. Lionel, save me!

BLANCHARD. It's done. You've been made a widow. Your husband, in God's view of time, died under my very eyes. He saw me. He laughed, and called out your name. Blood came out of his mouth, and your name was in it. He vomited the name back to me.

LUCILE. Lionel, listen!

BLANCHARD. He gave your body back as well. But too late.

ARMAND. Listen to her! Will you listen?

BLANCHARD. I know what she has to say. That she knew nothing and felt nothing, that I still have her faithful, uncontaminated soul. But today I'm a husband, and I'm not satisfied with these police court words. What I call a faithful wife is a wife who ceases to exist the moment a strange hand brushes against her. But the hand has touched my wife, taken hold of her, known her, and my wife is here, in health and spirits.

LUCILE. I was unconscious, Lionel.

ARMAND. What are you saying, Lucile?

BLANCHARD. Unconscious! That's even worse! I've been deceived by something deeper than the woman she is in the daytime, gossiping, housekeeping, shopping, the fully conscious woman that everybody knows; I've been deceived by the night-time in her, by the languid, naked sleep, which is what a man is most proud of when he's away from his wife. Leave here, Lucile, leave this house.

LUCILE. There's no need to ask me. I am going.

ARMAND. Lionel, listen to the truth.

LUCILE. Not a word, Armand. Do you hear? Don't say a word.

BLANCHARD. Get out of here, and don't play the victim. It's only too easy to be the victim! Here's a woman who doesn't drink wine, and even sips her quince-water with a certain anxiety, but who can't protect herself from drinking poison. She never loses a handkerchief or a key, she loses herself, and everything that my honour and happiness were made of, from her head to her foot, are swept past me to be squandered on this lecher Marcellus.

ARMAND. Lionel, question this woman here.

LIONEL. What a fool I've been, these five years, meekly going on respecting her virtue and innocence, respecting this body, if you please, when it refused every invitation from her husband, only to go and accept a lover. Oh, heavens, instead of all this, all this solemn high-thinking and timidity, what Marcellus-like nights I could have given myself!

LUCILE. There it is. It's over.

ARMAND. Lionel, you're beside yourself! Listen to me! Here is Barbette: it was her house that Lucile was carried off to. I do beg you. Question her.

LIONEL. So you were there, were you?

BARBETTE. Yes.

LIONEL. I'm listening.

BARBETTE. He undressed her.

ARMAND. What are you talking about, you liar?

BARBETTE. I say what I have to say, isn't that so, madam?

LUCILE. Yes. Thank you, Barbette.

LIONEL. And was she unconscious?

BARBETTE. Unconscious. She thanked him, and smiled, but unconsciously.

LIONEL. When he was leaving, what did she do?

BARBETTE. With her arms round his waist and his neck, she tried to hold him back, but unconsciously.

LIONEL. That's all there is to be said. (*Exit*)

ARMAND. Lionel, come back! The woman's lying! Lucile, please, you must call him back!

LUCILE. Thank you, Barbette.

ARMAND (*to* PAOLA). What are you smiling at?

PAOLA. One can smile. There stands Lucile, the woman.

BARBETTE. Well, I took your revenge for you, didn't I, my dear? That's what they're like. He's got his reward. He won't rest quiet again as long as he lives.

PAOLA. Well, Lucile, life is beautiful, is it, life is pure?

LUCILE. It's terrible. Everything is terrible.

PAOLA. Is there still the unbridgeable gulf between what you said was infamous, and what you described as noble?

ARMAND. Take no notice of her, Lucile. For the sake of the future, scorn to listen to her.

PAOLA. The future? There are two possible futures lying in front of Madame Blanchard today. The first is what she calls virtue. She is still obstinate enough, in spite of her downfall, to pick herself up again, and go on like a hypocrite with her career as the magistrate's wife.

ARMAND. And the other future is yours, is it not?

PAOLA. It's mine, it's love: and she would be foolish not to accept it. Anyway the battle is over, and I've won it; and victory is the only virtue there is in the world. Come, Barbette.

LUCILE. Get down on your knees, Paola!

PAOLA. On my knees?

LUCILE. On your knees! To ask a pardon.

PAOLA. To ask pardon of whom?

LUCILE. Of Marcellus. Of our husbands. Of Barbette. Of everyone alive or dead. Of me. Of yourself.

PAOLA. Pardon for what?

LUCILE. For having said that life is without worth or purity.

PAOLA. Well, isn't it? What worth can you see in today, for instance?

LUCILE. Today is horrible. It has mocked at everything, made everything vile.

PAOLA. Then we're in complete agreement, Lucile. It's a defeat for you, and there's no way out of it.

LUCILE. No way out of it? How wrong you are! The way out is here, in my hand. I went for help to a little girl, of my own age and my own name, who swore, when she was ten years old, never to accept evil, swore to prove, even by death if it had to be, that the world was a noble place, and that human beings were pure in heart. Now this world has become empty and terrible to her, and life nothing but corruption; but it doesn't matter, it isn't even true, because she is still going to keep the vow she swore.

BARBETTE. What are you doing? Why do you say this?

PAOLA. What has the little idiot done?

ARMAND. Lucile!

LUCILE. Don't call. There's no cure for this. The Thomasse murder has been good to me. I knew that the poison killed, and without any suffering. And quickly.

BARBETTE. Who made you do it, my poor little one? You weren't in any danger from men, I can tell you that. You were no concern of theirs, you were like an angel.

LUCILE. Armand!

ARMAND. Lucile.

LUCILE. My last wish, Armand! That my husband never knows the truth. Let him believe Barbette. He will live from now on scorning an innocent woman, as she has been scorning him: and admiring the guilty woman who hated life. He will live in a false legend, but what legends are true? Truth is always the poor lamb being sacrificed. What else could I have done, Armand? What else except play the heroine? Heroes are men who glorify a life which they can't bear any longer. And so it has come about with me. Is Paola kneeling?

PAOLA. Yes.

LUCILE. She is still standing, but she said yes. I have won. The world has purity, Paola, beauty, and light. Tell me so yourself. I want to hear you say so. Tell me quickly.

PAOLA. It is true . . . for this moment.

LUCILE. I'm content with that. A moment will do. Thank you.

Don't let Paola come near me. Barbette will dress me for burial.

(*She slips to the ground*)

PAOLA. She was called Lucrece, was she not?

(ARMAND *leads her away*)
(LUCILE *dies. The lights darken, and when they grow bright again* BARBETTE *is alone with* LUCILE)

BARBETTE.   Dear little creature, my little angel! The others have gone, and now we can talk. There's only God between us, and he has been with you since yesterday. If you had seen how you got up from the bed at midnight, you would know. It was a miracle . . . All the women in the town are talking about it already. You crossed yourself, and your stockings drew themselves on by themselves. Your shoes slipped themselves on to your feet. People have been canonized for less. The flowers I'd put at the bedside, my paper flowers, they breathed out the scent of roses, and when I went to touch them the flowers and the leaves were real. I'm not lying, I promise you; and just let me take this little ring off your finger to keep as a memory of it. You're thinner than you were yesterday, my angel: the ring comes off of its own accord. Mind you, miracles don't make our job any easier: they are bad for business. Purity's not for this world, but every ten years we get a gleam of it. And now all of them, with their intrigues and wicked doings, are going to see themselves standing in the light of it. Standing stock still, looking surprised, as though the photographer was taking them, as though the pure light was drenching their bodies. They will suddenly see it for the holy thing it was, and they'll feel it reproach them . . . It won't last long with them, I know that very well. With women the virtue of one is the virtue of all. Whereas each man lives the lord of his own dunghill, and has to be his own saint, and his own purgatory. Get along with you. We've all understood you; Paola as much as anybody. It's true you were ravished. But not by Marcellus. You could have got over that, fifty women have got over that; you knew yourself you could. But what struck you down was being made aware of man's stupidity, and coarseness, and wickedness, too much all of a sudden. And if you're as tender a creature as you, you die of it. Your brooch is coming undone; that means you're giving it to me, and I'm taking it for a keepsake. There's only this mark of the bite my old mouth gave you that you'll have to explain up there, but don't think twice about it. Show it to them, explain. Tell them it's a kiss to all women from an old bawd in Aix, and you've brought it along as a promise from her that she, and all her sisters of the town, won't give men any rest, neither in the profession nor on the side, neither to the young ones who snigger like fools, nor the old ones with their lecherous grinning, nor the handsome ones, nor the ugly ones, nor the city treasurer, nor the magistrate's clerk who comes as a spy: give no rest to their health, nor their purse, nor their family, nor the marrow of their bones, so as to revenge you, my little angel, and lead them all straight to eternal damnation. Amen.

THE CURTAIN FALLS

Date Due

70
71
72
74
75
76
77
79
80
85